# Ancient Privileges:
# *Beowulf,* Law,
# and the Making of
# Germanic Antiquity

*by*

## Stefan Jurasinski

WEST VIRGINIA UNIVERSITY PRESS
MORGANTOWN 2006

West Virginia University Press, Morgantown 26506
© 2006 by West Virginia University Press

First edition published 2006 by West Virginia University Press
Printed in the United States of America

13 12 11 10 09 08 07 06    9 8 7 6 5 4 3 2 1

ISBN 0-937058-98-X (alk. paper)

Library of Congress Cataloguing-in-Publication Data

Ancient Privileges. Beowulf, Law,
and the Making of Germanic Antiquity / Stefan Jurasinski.
p. cm. – (Medieval European Studies ; 6)
1. Social history Medieval, 500-1500. 2. English Literature–Old English,
ca. 450-1100–History and criticism. 3. Civilization, Medieval, in literature.
4. Germanic literature–History and criticism. 5. Germanic philology.
6. Philologists–Germany–Biography. 7. Beowulf–Editing. I. Title. II.
Jurasinski, Stefan. III. Series.

IN PROCESS

Library of Congress Control Number: 2005937638

Printed in USA by Lightning Source.
Typeset by Than Saffel.
Cover image by Lazlo Matulay and published in *By His Own Might: The
Battles of Beowulf* by Dorothy Hosford (Holt, Rinehart and Winston, 1947).

# Contents

# Abbreviations

| | |
|---|---|
| *ASE* | *Anglo-Saxon England* |
| ASPR | Anglo-Saxon Poetic Records |
| EETS | Early English Text Society |
| *JEGP* | *Journal of English and Germanic Philology* |
| MGH | Monumenta Germaniæ Historica |
| *MP* | *Modern Philology* |
| *PQ* | *Philological Quarterly* |
| *PMLA* | *Publications of the Modern Language Association* |
| *RES* | *Review of English Studies* |
| Liebermann, ed., *Gesetze* | Felix Liebermann, ed. and trans. *Die Gesetze der Angelsachsen.* 3 vols. Halle: Max Niemeyer, 1903-16. |
| Klaeber, ed., *Beowulf* | Fr. Klaeber, ed. *Beowulf and the Fight at Finnsburg.* 3rd ed., with first and second supplements. Lexington, MA: Heath, 1950. |
| Tacitus, *Germania* | *Cornelii Taciti Opera Minora*, eds. M. Winterbottom and R. M. Ogilvie. Oxford: Clarendon, 1975. |

# Preface

THIS STUDY CONSIDERS the influence of nineteenth-century legal historians on the editing and interpretation of *Beowulf.* It is both a contribution to the study of Anglo-Saxonism and an attempt to historicize the assumptions that *Beowulf* criticism habitually employs regarding the legal setting of the poem. Since a number of the doctrines explored within this study have undergone no critical analysis for several decades, I have occasionally not been able to avoid offering new arguments regarding the nature of Germanic legal practices that have significant implications for how we read *Beowulf.* This is especially the case in my discussion of the nature of liability for accidental homicide in Germanic legal sources.

Portions of this study have been published elsewhere. An earlier version of chapter 2 appeared in the *Journal of English and Germanic Philology* 103 (2004), 323-40, and an earlier version of chapter 3 appeared in the *Review of English Studies* n.s. 55 (2004), 641–61. I am indebted to the editors of these journals for permission to reprint and recast work. A much briefer version of chapter 4 was presented at the 39th annual International Congress on Medieval Studies at Western Michigan University, and I am grateful to the audience for their insightful questions and comments.

Naturally I have incurred a number of debts in the process of completing this work, which began as a doctoral dissertation submitted at Indiana University in 2003. I am grateful to the members of the committee—Alfred David, R. D. Fulk, Kari Ellen Gade, and Emanuel Mickel, Jr.—for their enthusiasm for the project throughout its development. For their extraordinary generosity and invaluable guidance, I owe particular debts to R.D. Fulk and Kari Ellen Gade. Any errors of fact or interpretation that may remain in this study are, of course, my responsibility alone. All translations are my own unless otherwise indicated, though Professor Gade helped me on many occasions to arrive at more accurate and more idiomatic translations from Modern German.

I would also like to acknowledge a debt to Charles Wright, whose comments on an earlier version of chapter 2 made its argument significantly more persuasive. The two reviewers for West Virginia University Press also offered many helpful recommendations that I have incorporated into this study. I am especially grateful to Patrick Conner for his interest in the project. His comments on the manuscript saved me from a number of errors and corrected some instances of awkward phrasing.

Finally I would like to thank my wife, Aurora, whose wisdom, humor and patience have sustained me throughout the course of this project.

# INTRODUCTION:
## "THE FORESTS OF GERMANY": LEGAL HISTORY AND THE INHERITANCE OF PHILOLOGY

THE LAST TWO DECADES have seen a proliferation of books and articles concerned with the historical and cultural background of contemporary Old English studies. Indeed, the study of Anglo-Saxonism has reached such a degree of popularity that one could be forgiven for thinking that the desire to historicize the discipline is a new development. Of course it is not: two biographies of John Mitchell Kemble have been available to scholars for several decades, as have Berkhout and Gatch's classic anthology of essays on the origins of Anglo-Saxon scholarship and Hans Aarsleff's invaluable history of eighteenth- and nineteenth-century theories of language.[1] It probably cannot be said that we know a great deal more about the origins of Old English scholarship than we did twenty or thirty years ago, though recently the labors of Robert Bjork and T. A. Shippey have made available to English-speaking audiences a wealth of

---

[1] See Bruce Dickins, "John Mitchell Kemble and Old English Scholarship," *Proceedings of the British Academy* 25 (1939), pp. 51-84; Raymond A. Wiley, *Anglo-Saxon Kemble: the Life and Works of John Mitchell Kemble, 1807-1857: Philologist, Historian and Archaeologist,* Anglo-Saxon Studies in Archaeology and History 1 (Oxford: B.A.R., 1979); idem, ed. and trans., *John Mitchell Kemble and Jakob Grimm: A Correspondence 1832-1852* (Leiden: E. J. Brill, 1971); *Anglo-Saxon Scholarship: The First Three Centuries,* eds. Carl T. Berkhout and Milton McC. Gatch (Boston, MA: G. K. Hall, 1982); Hans Aarsleff, *The Study of Language in England 1780-1860* (Princeton, N.J.: Princeton Univ. Press, 1967). A useful overview of Old English scholarship in the eighteenth and nineteenth centuries can be found in T. A. Birrell, "The Society of Antiquaries and the Taste for Old English 1705-1840," *Neophilologus* 50 (1966), pp. 107–11.

important and heretofore untranslated scholarship from Germany and Scandinavia.[2]

What is new is the perspective with which knowledge about the origins of English philology is sought and deployed in contemporary scholarship. Particularly in the last decade, research into the beginnings of English philology has been preoccupied with how the emergence of this field coincided with the development of nationalist and imperialist ideologies in England, Germany, Scandinavia and the United States.[3] According to Allen Frantzen, the literary remains of Anglo-Saxon civilization were used by scholars like Kemble to establish myths of national origin supportive of imperialist ideology. The customs and beliefs attested in the surviving monuments of literate culture were held to represent the infancy of English society; accordingly, demonstrating their continuity with present-day institutions was one of the duties of the philologist and the historian:

> Kemble, Turner and Macaulay represented different historical
> methods, but they shared important assumptions about English

[2] Robert Bjork, "Nineteenth-Century Scandinavia and the Birth of Anglo-Saxon Studies," in *Anglo-Saxonism and the Construction of Social Identity*, eds. Allen Frantzen and John D. Niles (Gainesville: Univ. Press of Florida, 1997), pp. 111-32; *Beowulf: The Critical Heritage*, eds. and trans. T. A. Shippey and Andreas Haarder (London: Routledge, 1998).

[3] A representative sampling of such works includes Clare Simmons's excellent *Reversing the Conquest: History and Myth in Nineteenth-Century British Literature* (New Brunswick: Rutgers Univ. Press, 1990); Allen Frantzen, *Desire for Origins: New Language, Old English and Teaching the Tradition* (New Brunswick: Rutgers Univ. Press, 1990); *Literary Appropriations of the Anglo-Saxons from the Thirteenth to the Twentieth Century*, eds. D. G. Scragg and Carole Weinberg (Cambridge: Cambridge Univ. Press, 2000); María José Mora and María José Gómez-Calderón, "The Study of Old English in America (1776-1850): National Uses of the Saxon Past," *JEGP* 97 (1998), pp. 322-36; María José Mora, "The Invention of the Old English Elegy," *English Studies* 76 (1995), pp. 129-39.

history. They viewed England's medieval past as the nation's childhood, grasped the importance of the Anglo-Saxon—that is, Germanic—past as a foundation for contemporary claims to supremacy, saw scholarly discipline as essential to proper understanding of the past, and accepted as the historian's chief duty the commemoration of the nation's greatness. They saw the past as primitive, little more than a rudimentary version of the present, without values of its own; if they idealized childhood, they left no doubt that primitivism, whether cultural or chronological, was ideal only after progress transcended it.[4]

Frantzen later demonstrates the persistence of nineteenth-century discourses about cultural origins in major subfields of contemporary literary research such as stemmatology, reconstructive textual editing and source criticism.[5] His aim is not to delegitimize these methods but to make Old English specialists self-conscious of the rhetorical strategies underlying the aura of objectivity that philological approaches to literature have historically assumed. Kemble's work on Old English is customarily seen as inaugurating for English-speaking scholars an era of scientific inquiry into the language and its literary monuments.[6] Yet Kemble's assumptions, as Frantzen and others have demonstrated, were necessarily conditioned by the prevailing attitudes of his historical moment. The methods he brought to the study of the early Germanic languages demonstrably possessed ideological affiliations that are effaced by routine references to his approach as "scientific" or objective.[7]

The contribution for which Kemble is most famous (or notorious) is his introduction of English-speaking scholars to the

---

[4] Frantzen, *Desire for Origins,* pp. 56-57.

[5] Frantzen, *Desire for Origins,* pp. 62-98.

[6] Frantzen, *Desire for Origins,* pp. 57-58.

[7] Similar arguments were made two decades ago by Elmer Antonsen, "Linguistics and Politics in the 19th Century: The Case of the 15th Rune," *Michigan Germanic Studies* 6 (1980), pp. 1-16.

methods of linguistic analysis pioneered in Grimm's *Deutsche Grammatik* (1819-37). This undertaking unfortunately involved Kemble in a series of belligerent exchanges with the representatives of an English scholarly establishment whose traditions were, as they saw it, menaced by Grimm's innovations.[8] The most well-known of Grimm's discoveries—though the credit undoubtedly belongs to Rasmus Rask—is the First Consonant Shift, which established the descent of the Germanic languages from Indo-European through a regular series of sound changes. On the basis of the resemblance between words such as Old English *fisc* and Latin *piscis*, a common original could be posited in the manner of early nineteenth-century biologists who were already experimenting with the notion of evolution.[9]

As Richard Marggraf Turley has observed, the passage of time has obscured the political ramifications of this discovery, which were immense in an environment that had held European vernaculars to be inferior to Latin and Greek, the real languages of learning. Indeed, Turley contends that the political significance of claims made in Grimm's *Grammatik* may have played a greater role than their scientific merits in overcoming the initially vehement resistance of the English scholarly establishment. "Read in a certain way," Turley states, "[Grimm's *Grammatik*] seemed to offer a means of navigating the impasse of traditional linguistic genealogies that had favoured Latin and Greek over English . . . In Grimm's relational schema, words such as 'piscis' and 'fish' were revealed as, to all extents and purposes, identical.

---

[8] An excellent overview appears in Raymond A. Wiley, "Grimm's Grammar Gains Ground in England," in *The Grimm Brothers and the Germanic Past*, Studies in the History of the Language Sciences 54, ed. Elmer Antonsen (Philadelphia: John Benjamins, 1990), pp. 33-42.

[9] See Maria Dobozy, "The Brothers Grimm: Jacob Ludwig Carl (1785-1863); Wilhelm Carl (1786-1859)," in *Medieval Scholarship: Biographical Studies on the Formation of a Discipline, vol. 2: Literature and Philology*, ed. Helen Damico (New York: Garland, 1998), pp. 93-108 at p. 97.

Latin could not be a 'better' language than English, and thus Roman culture no better than its English counterpart."[10] What such developments ultimately offered to English philological scholarship was a means of

> dismantling the myths of Latin and Greek as linguistic patri-
> archs, while simultaneously adhering to the terms of the old-
> er, pre-morphological study in order to reappraise northern
> tongues such as English more favourably.[11]

Turley's study is a caution to anyone who would believe that philological "science" (or any other mode of inquiry that claims objectivity for itself) can remain aloof from the influence of ideology. Indeed, discomfort with the notion of scientific or objective scholarship characterizes much of the recent interest in the early history of Old English studies. Published in the same year as Frantzen's *Desire for Origins*, Clare Simmons's *Reversing the Conquest* considers the major texts of Victorian historiography alongside contemporaneous works of historical fiction. Simmons argues that the two performed the same ideological work: "Ultimately, the relationship between 'scholarship' and 'literature' had to be a reciprocal one . . . [O]nly in a society that had already accepted the characterization of its ancestors created by the 'serious scholars' could novelists present popularized characterizations of Saxons and Normans."[12] Like Frantzen, Simmons is concerned throughout much of her study to problematize the distinction between "objective" history and fictional narrative. Though the nineteenth century saw the advent of history as a "fact-controlling discipline" whose first aim was to separate real events from story, Victorian historiography

---

[10] Richard Marggraf Turley, *The Politics of Language in Romantic Literature* (New York: Palgrave MacMillan, 2002), pp. 133-34.

[11] Turley, *The Politics of Language in Romantic Literature*, p. 134.

[12] Simmons, *Reversing the Conquest*, pp. 70-71.

replaced the narratives in which it had found its materials with a dominant narrative of its own.[13] All events of English history were held to represent a nearly unbroken continuity of customs and traditions.

What Simmons calls the "nineteenth-century claim to historical continuity" of course has certain affinities with earlier conceptions of English history.[14] J. G. A. Pocock has famously documented the survival of the "common law mind" from Sir Edward Coke through Edmund Burke, a peculiarly English faith in the unbroken continuity of the "ancient constitution" from antiquity to the modern era.[15] The widespread tendency to privilege customary over innovative practices established a rhetoric of custom that was even appropriated by the rural poor and their advocates during the movement to enclose common grazing areas. Thomas Andrews's *Enquiry into the Causes of the Encrease and Miseries of the Poor of England* (1738) rails against landowners for excluding the poor from unenclosed commons through the use of "stints" or restrictions on the number of grazing animals that might feed in common areas, claiming that by such measures the "Ancient Privileges" of the rural poor "are taken away and given to the *Rich*."[16] As E. P. Thompson notes, the tendency to imagine the right of common as immemorial custom was already in place in the thirteenth century; the ubiquity of

[13] Simmons, *Reversing the Conquest,* p. 13.

[14] Simmons, *Reversing the Conquest,* p. 14.

[15] J.G.A. Pocock, *The Ancient Constitution and the Feudal Law* (Cambridge: Cambridge Univ. Press 1957; Reissue with Retrospect, 1987), pp. 255-305 and *passim.*

[16] Quoted in Leigh Shaw-Taylor, "Labourers, Cows, Common Rights and Parliamentary Enclosure: The Evidence of Contemporary Comment c. 1760-1810," *Past and Present* 171 (2001), pp. 95-126 at p. 126. W. E. Tate discusses the problematic attempts to adduce the fairly equivocal statements in chapter 26 of Tacitus's *Germania* as evidence for the right of common: see his *Enclosure Movement* (New York: Walker and Co., 1967), pp. 40-41.

the claim says as much about the importance of the invocation of custom as a rhetorical device as it does about the institution of common agriculture itself.[17]

The emergence of two new sciences in the nineteenth-century—comparative philology and evolutionary biology—permitted the belief in immemorial custom to be articulated in ways that emphasized its supposed basis in historical and scientific fact. Comparative philology had established the descent of English from a common stock of Germanic dialects, while evolutionary biology imbued the historical imagination of the nineteenth century with a faith in continual progress.[18] These circumstances, combined with the new tendency of historians to present themselves as disinterested interpreters of historical phenomena, permanently changed the way in which scholars imagined immemorial custom. Speaking to students at Cambridge in 1895, Lord Acton claimed that the importance of history as a mode of inquiry consisted in its ability to reveal the values of the present in the remains of the remote past: "[I]n society, as in nature, the structure is continuous, and we can trace things back uninterruptedly, until we dimly perceive the Declaration of Independence in the forests of Germany."[19] Writing in 1876, Henry Adams had used nearly identical language to describe the state of professional legal-historical study:

[17] See E. P. Thompson, *Customs in Common* (New York: The New Press, 1993), p. 104; see also Jean Birrell, "Common Rights in the Medieval Forest," *Past and Present* 117 (1987), p. 29. This is certainly not to imply that such rights did not exist. What is of interest here is the way in which an existing rhetoric of immemorial custom could be appropriated by advocates of the poor because of its conventional status within political and legal argumentation.

[18] For a fuller discussion of the effects of this development on legal history (and ultimately the interpretation of *Beowulf*) see chapters 3 and 4 below.

[19] Lord Acton [John Emerich Edward Darlberg], *A Lecture on the Study of History, Delivered at Cambridge June 11 1895* (London: Macmillan, 1895), p. 2; quoted in Simmons, *Reversing the Conquest*, p. 6.

The student of history who now attempts to trace, through two thousand years of vicissitudes and dangers, the slender thread of political and legal thought, no longer loses it from sight in the confusion of feudalism, or the wild lawlessness of the Heptarchy, but follows it safely and firmly back until it leads him out upon the wide plains of northern Germany, and attaches itself at last to the primitive popular assembly, parliament, law-court, and army in one; which embraced every free man, rich or poor, and in theory at least allowed equal rights to all.[20]

Adams's observations further illustrate how arbitrary the distinction between scholarship and fiction might be in the nineteenth century. Somber invocations of the mythical "forests of Germany" by nineteenth-century historians indicate both the degree to which their newly-professionalized "fact controlling discipline" remained dependent upon story, and the degree to which the "science" of philology (itself dependent upon the evolutionist language of natural science) was able to give a fresh appearance of credibility to the slumbering myth of the "ancient constitution" that had once sustained the earliest historians of law before falling into widespread disfavor. For once comparative philology had made knowledge of their Anglo-Saxon ancestors more reliable and scientific than ever before, scholars interested in the development of the law no longer had to locate the origins of legal customs in the proverbial "time out of mind" or in the era of Brutus.[21] A wealth of legal and literary

---

[20] Henry Adams, "The Anglo-Saxon Courts of Law," in *Essays in Anglo-Saxon Law*, eds. H. Adams *et al.* (Boston: Little, Brown and Co., 1876 repr. 1905), p. 1. Samuel Kliger finds similar sentiments from the seventeenth and eighteenth centuries in his *Goths in England* (Cambridge, MA: Harvard Univ. Press, 1952), p. 27.

[21] Kliger (*Goths in England,* chap. 1 and *passim*) documents the rise of a parallel tradition to Pocock's "common-law mind" in the widespread belief in the "Gothic" origins of England's democratic institutions. This

texts were for the first time appearing in reliable editions, and a number of scholars took the suggestions of historians like Acton literally, hoping to find in these texts the seeds of modern institutions. Their efforts would be qualitatively different from those of eighteenth-century scholars such as Blackstone, one of the first legal scholars whose genealogy of English law would reflect centuries of sporadic work on the legislative remains of Anglo-Saxon England. While it is true that Blackstone goes further than his predecessors in making Alfred's code the fount of English legal tradition, the *Commentaries* most likely reflect the after-effects of Alfred's twelfth-century apotheosis as England's Solomonic lawgiver more than any philological discoveries.[22] Blackstone spoke of the legislation of King Edward the Confessor (which few at the time suspected was a forgery) as a "digest" not unlike that of Justinian.[23] He brought to pre-Conquest ma-

tradition can be traced to the sixteenth century and likewise held that the continuity of Gothic freedoms was unbroken by the Norman Conquest. Pocock acknowledges that these two traditions constituted "two different, if intermingled, lines of intellectual development" that were sometimes "blithely combined and confused by persons unaware of the different foundations on which each rested" (Pocock, *Ancient Constitution and the Feudal Law*, p. 57). Certainly the acceptance of modern comparative philology within England only added to this confusion.

[22] William Blackstone, *Commentaries on the Laws of England. A Facsimile of the First Edition of 1765-1769*, 4 vols. (Chicago: Univ. of Chicago Press, 1979), I, 66. On the apotheosis of Alfred after the Conquest the best overviews remain E. G. Stanley, *Die angelsächsische Rechtspflege und wie man sie später aufgefaßt hat* (Munich: Verlag der Bayerischen Akademie der Wissenschaften, 1999) and Simon Keynes, "The Cult of King Alfred the Great," *ASE* 28 (1999), pp. 225-356. The role of the thirteenth-century *Mirror of Justices* in establishing the veneration of Alfred as a *topos* of early modern legal history is crucial: see my "Andrew Horn, Alfredian Apocrypha, and the Anglo-Saxon Names of the *Mirror of Justices*" (forthcoming, *Journal of English and Germanic Philology*).

[23] Blackstone, *Commentaries*, p. 66.

terials no specialized hermeneutic or ethnographic principles that he would not have applied to any other body of legislation. The notion of law as something inherent in the language and culture of a people had yet to be developed.[24] Accordingly, his interests did not extend to any normative statements attested outside of legislation.

The exclusive focus of legal historians on tracing the development of English law would not survive the development by Grimm and his descendants in comparative philology of new analytical categories that would render all such pursuits nearly impossible. That the historical study of the grammars of discrete Northern European languages would ultimately be overshadowed by the study of "Germanic" became clear in Kemble's unpublished panegyric on Grimm's *Grammatik*. Kemble described the *Grammatik* as "a grammar of the Teutonic languages, or, as it would be better to say, a grammar of the *Teutonic language;* a complex of the laws, which, as they prevail in all the dialects,

---

[24] This development is dated by Wormald (*The Making of English Law: King Alfred to the Twelfth Century,* vol. 1. [Oxford: Blackwell, 1999], p. 11) to the late eighteenth and early nineteenth century, and is held to be inseparable from the discovery of Indo-European as the progenitor of most European languages: "The revelation that a common 'Indo-European' language was spoken from the Ganges to the North Cape created an irresistible impression that law, hardly less basic to human sociability, could spread to all corners of the world, yet retain its essential identity." The hypothesis that the law behaves much like language in the cultural life of the folk is central to work undertaken by the tradition of legal-historical scholarship known as the *historische Rechtsschule,* and shows the lingering influence of the nineteenth-century philological tradition within which it was born: see Ruth Schmidt-Wiegand, "Das sinnliche Element des Rechts. Jakob Grimms Sammlung und Beschreibung deutscher Rechtsaltertümer," in *Kasseler Vorträge in Erinnerung an den 200. Geburtstag der brüder Jacob und Wilhelm Grimm,* Schriften der Brüder Grimm-Gesellschaft Kassel e.V. 19, ed. Ludwig Denecke (Marburg: Elwert, 1988), pp. 6-8 and *passim.*

may perhaps, without any great impropriety, be called the *Essential language.*[25] And though history has not been kind to Kemble's opponents in English philology, it is hard not to see in the implications of such comments a very real basis for their misgivings about the triumph of Germanic as a linguistic and cultural category. It is true that such methodological innovations made possible the elevation of English to a status once enjoyed by Greek or Latin within the cultural value hierarchy to which most West Europeans implicitly subscribed. Yet much was lost as well. All that was peculiar to the development of each Germanic-speaking nation was to diminish in value. All effects of cultural exchange with non-Germanic peoples and all the influences of Christian teaching were to be viewed as contaminants.[26]

Students of Old English literature live perhaps more than most who work in fields descended from nineteenth-century philology in the wake of this development. Its influence on scholarly attempts to make sense of *Beowulf* over the centuries has yet to be fully explored. Contemporary scholarship rarely acknowledges that *Beowulf* played a central role in the effort to reconstruct the primitive Germanic legal system, a circumstance made possible by the view, widespread throughout much of its modern reception, that the poem's value inhered chiefly in its status as a historical rather than literary artifact. James Harrison's "Old Teutonic Life in Beowulf" (1884), an article of which Klaeber evidently had a high opinion, is in many ways a typical expression of faith in the poem's ability to reveal the origins of later English legal practices:

[25] John Mitchell Kemble, *John Mitchell Kemble's Review of Jakob Grimm's Deutsche Grammatik,* Old English Newsletter *Subsidia* 6 (Binghamton, NY: CEMERS, SUNY-Binghamton, 1981), p. 4.

[26] On this see especially E. G. Stanley, *In the Foreground:* Beowulf (Woodbridge: D.S. Brewer, 1994), p. 219: "For two centuries or so, and still occasionally, Germanic scholars, many of them in real life mild bookish people at their desks, have sought out as their favourites, not the Christian verities in Anglo-Saxon poems, but rather the Teutonic antiquities."

The political aspects mirrored in Beowulf are of great interest. We find kings surrounded by their thanes; an hereditary dynasty with its hereditary castle; a court in which are prescribed forms. . . . There are minstrels; folc-land, hereditary estates (*êthel*, 1520), and hereditary prerogative (2199) are spoken of . . . The elective principle prevails; there are wars, alliances, feuds. Great stress is laid upon kin, kinship—that atom out of which has developed all society. We see the consanguine eddy already at work, concentrating or scattering communities which were to grow into shires and kingdoms. Blood-relationship is the root which develops into a stem, into a folk, into a nation.[27]

One of a generation of scholars whom Tolkien chided for considering *Beowulf* "a manual of Germanic antiquities," Harrison held that the worth of the poem as historical evidence was due primarily to the archaism of its contents.[28] For him, *Beowulf* was "a sort of poetic *Germania:* an unconscious poetic treatise on the customs and habits of the early Germans at once confirmatory of and supplementary to Tacitus."[29] Views such as these maintained a surprising tenacity and persisted well past the turn of the century. Archibald Strong's *Short History of English Literature* (1921) contended that "*Beowulf* is the picture of a whole civilization, of the Germania which Tacitus describes. The main interest which the poem has for us is thus

[27] James A. Harrison, "Old Teutonic Life in Beowulf," *The Overland Monthly* n.s. 4 (1884), pp. 14-24, 152-61 at p. 160. Klaeber includes the essay in his bibliography on "Old Germanic Life;" See Klaeber, ed., *Beowulf*, pp. clxxvi-clxxvii. All quotations from *Beowulf* throughout this study are drawn from Klaeber's edition unless otherwise indicated.

[28] J. R. R. Tolkien, "Beowulf: The Monsters and the Critics," *Proceedings of the British Academy* 22 (1936), pp. 245-95, repr. in Fulk, ed., *Interpretations of Beowulf*, pp. 14-44 at p. 16.

[29] Harrison, "Old Teutonic Life in Beowulf," p. 16.

not a purely literary interest. *Beowulf* is an important historical document."[30]

Claims such as those of Harrison and Strong are rarely taken seriously in contemporary studies of *Beowulf.* A number of scholars now locate the date of composition close to the preparation of the manuscript.[31] Even those who accept an earlier date are far less likely than previous generations to find the poem's contents Tacitean.[32] Yet the claims underlying many attempts to use *Beowulf* as a source of legal-historical evidence endure in contemporary editions and scholarly discussions of the poem. With respect to its discussion of land tenure, for example, Harrison's essay contains little with which standard editions of *Beowulf* would incline us to disagree. The distinction between *folcland* and *eðel* (or communal and hereditary land, respectively) was first advanced by Kemble in 1849, and is endorsed by the editions of

---

[30] Archibald Strong, *A Short History of English Literature* (London: Oxford Univ. Press, 1921), pp. 2-3.

[31] Some of the most influential discussions of dating occur in *The Dating of Beowulf,* ed. Colin Chase (Toronto: Univ. of Toronto Press, 1980), a milestone of *Beowulf* scholarship that lent a new credibility to arguments for a date closer to the preparation of the manuscript (though contributors such as Clemoes and Pope argued against this proposition). Kevin Kiernan likewise argues for a date close to he preparation of the manuscript in his *Beowulf and the Beowulf Manuscript* (Ann Arbor, MI: Univ. of Michigan Press, 1997). For a dissenting view, see R. D. Fulk, "Review Article: Dating *Beowulf* to the Viking Age," *PQ* 61 (1982), pp. 341-59. The strongest evidence yet for an early eighth-century date is presented in Michael Lapidge, "The Archetype of Beowulf," *Anglo-Saxon England* 29 (2000), pp. 5-41.

[32] Contemporary scholarship has grown much more doubtful of the usefulness of the *Germania* for the interpretation of Old English texts. See especially M. J. Toswell, "Tacitus, Old English Heroic Poetry, and Ethnographic Preconceptions," in *'Doubt Wisely:' Papers in Honour of E. G. Stanley* (London: Routledge, 1996), pp. 493-507.

Klaeber and Wrenn.[33] Yet as a working concept in the field of Anglo-Saxon legal history, the distinction did not survive the turn of the century: few if any contemporary legal historians understand *folcland* as "common land," though the equivalence was self-evident to Kemble and his contemporaries. As the following chapters will show, nineteenth-century speculations on the nature of Germanic law are often responsible for the most widely accepted readings of the poem's major episodes and most difficult cruces.

In cataloguing and examining such survivals of nineteenth-century thought my purpose is twofold. First, I would like to subject these claims to the sort of reevaluation from which they have been relatively safe for nearly a century. Second, I would like to provide specialists in Old English with a sense of how profoundly the editing and criticism of the poem were once affected by the study of legal history. It is difficult to understand how our present understanding of *Beowulf* can have remained untouched by modern research in legal history without some sense of how the concerns of literary and legal-historical scholarship grew so disparate. Accordingly, the following section contains a brief sketch of how law is implicated in the development of Germanic philology.

## LAW AND PHILOLOGY

In part because of Klaeber's dependence on works like Kemble's *Saxons in England* (1849) for a picture of *Beowulf*'s social environment, and the habits this choice appears to have engendered in subsequent scholarship, it is fair to say that a century of research in the field of legal history—from Pollock and Maitland's *History of English Law* (1898) and Vinogradoff's *Villainage in England* (1892) to Wormald's *Making of English Law* (1999)—has hardly begun to affect the study of the poem. The pressures of departmentalization, and the changes effected by

[33] See chapter 2 for a full bibliography.

14

this movement upon the scholarly environment within which texts like *Beowulf* are studied, certainly bear much of the responsibility.

One of the distinctive features of nineteenth-century philology as an academic discipline was the catholicity of its interests. Throughout the nineteenth century this was a feature of philological study about which its protagonists were especially proud. Albert Cook's address to the 1897 MLA convention typifies the boundless faith of many nineteenth-century scholars in the potential of philology:

> The function of the philologist . . . is the endeavor to relive the life of the past; to enter by the imagination into the spiritual experiences of all the historic protagonists of civilization in a given period and area of culture; to think the thoughts, to feel the emotions, to partake the aspirations, recorded in literature; to become one with humanity in the struggles of a given nation or race to perceive and attain the ideal of existence . . . [he] is at once antiquary, palaeographer, grammarian, lexicologist, expounder, critic, historian of literature, and, above all, lover of humanity.[34]

The interest of philology in all written remains of earlier civilizations, and not strictly literary texts, remains a significant feature of contemporary philological work in the Germanic languages. Specialists in Old English still approach the study of legal texts differently from their counterparts in other fields. For example, scholars specializing in Middle English rarely address themselves solely to the legislation and court records of the fourteenth and fifteenth centuries.[35]

[34] Albert C. Cook, "The Province of English Philology," repr. in *PMLA* 115 (2000), pp. 1742-43 at p. 1742.

[35] According to Richard Firth Green, an additional reason why post-conquest legal records have received little attention from literary scholars in comparison to Anglo-Saxon legislation is that post-conquest records

Where they do so, the strategy is primarily undertaken in "law and literature" studies, where legislative evidence serves the larger aim of disclosing the dominant ideologies and cultural norms adumbrated by literary texts.[36] In Old English scholarship, however, there remains a sporadic but persistent tradition of addressing legal matters independently of literature.[37] It is hard not to imagine that the confidence with which some specialists in Germanic philology approach legal-historical problems can be traced to the belief that knowledge of language constitutes knowledge of law—that the law is in some sense embedded in language.[38] Such an assumption constitutes a distinct and insufficiently appreciated inheritance of contemporary Anglo-Saxon studies from the late eighteenth and early nineteenth centuries. As Aarsleff has observed, the "rediscovery" of ancient languages in the modern era has almost always occurred under the aus-

are not predominantly in English and employ an often impenetrable jargon: see Richard Firth Green, "Medieval Literature and Law," in *The Cambridge History of Medieval Literature*, ed. David Wallace (Cambridge: Cambridge Univ. Press, 1999), pp. 407-31 at p. 408.

[36] A characteristic example is Bruce Holsinger, "Vernacular Legality: The English Jurisdictions of the Owl and the Nightingale," in *The Letter of the Law: Legal Practice and Literary Production in Medieval England*, eds. Emily Steiner and Candace Barrington (Ithaca, NY: Cornell Univ. Press, 2002), pp. 154-184.

[37] For some examples of this approach see Dorothy Bethurum, "Stylistic Features of the Old English Laws," *Modern Language Review* 27 (1932), pp. 263-279; Horst Haider Munske, *Der germanische Rechtswortschatz im Bereich der Missetaten*, vol. 1 (Berlin: Walter de Gruyter, 1973); Carole Hough, "The Early Kentish 'Divorce Laws': A Reconsideration of Aethelberht chs. 79 and 80," *ASE* 23 (1994), pp. 1-6; Lisi Oliver, "*Cyninges Fedesl:* The Feeding of the King in Aethelberht ch. 12," *ASE* 27 (1998), pp. 31-40. All of these studies apply the methods of comparative philology to legal-historical questions.

[38] See Wormald, *Making of English Law*, p. 11; Aarsleff, *Study of Language in England*, pp. 115-65

pices of attempts to reconstruct archaic legal systems.[39] Some of the first Old English materials to be satisfactorily edited were codes of royal legislation, and it might be said that the study of Old English was first undertaken as a means of recovering England's "ancient constitution" as well as the customs of the English Church.[40] During the first half of the nineteenth century, the study of law was not subordinated to the study of literature; indeed, many of the great nineteenth-century philologists devoted as much effort to the study of legal history as they did to linguistic or literary problems.

It is significant that Benjamin Thorpe, an early editor of *Beowulf*, worked with legal materials before attempting to edit the poem, producing an edition of Anglo-Saxon legislation which remained standard until the early twentieth century.[41] Jakob Grimm began his career as a student of Friedrich Carl von Savigny, a founder of modern legal-historical studies, and his work on the Germanic languages was largely a response to the latter's famous conviction that the *Volksgeist* was preserved in a nation's system of customary law.[42] Kemble was himself a student at the Inner Temple before moving to Göttingen, and his interest in the law never ceased.[43] In addition to his having produced the

---

[39] Aarsleff, *The Study of Language in England*, p. 119.

[40] See William Lambarde, ed. and trans., *Archaionomia* (1568: reprint, London: Roger Daniel, 1644); Richard Terrill, "William Lambarde: Elizabethan Humanist and Legal Historian," *Journal of Legal History* 6 (1985), pp. 157-178.

[41] Benjamin Thorpe, *Ancient Laws and Institutes of England* (London: Eyre and Spottiswoode, 1840). His edition of *Beowulf* did not appear until 1855.

[42] Aarsleff, *The Study of Language in England*, p. 119. See chapter 2 for a full discussion and bibliography.

[43] See the entry for John Mitchell Kemble in the *Dictionary of National Biography*, 22 vols., eds. Sir Leslie Stephen and Sir Sidney Lee (London: Oxford Univ. Press, 1949-50), IV, 1257-60 at p. 1270. The entry also contains a comprehensive bibliography of Kemble's published works.

first edition of *Beowulf* based on modern principles, Kemble is known to posterity through an achievement that has rarely been duplicated since: his comprehensive edition of Old English charters.

Only during the late nineteenth and early twentieth centuries did the study of Old English law and literature begin their more or less permanent bifurcation. Whereas the writings of Grimm and Kemble are replete with articles on law and Germanic institutions, discussions of non-literary texts are almost entirely absent from the writings of scholars such as Klaeber. The breach between Old English legal and literary studies, though not as profound as that of other fields, is crossed less often now than it was during the nineteenth century. That it is crossed at all is probably due to some philologists' continued awareness of themselves as inheritors of a scholarly tradition whose interests once extended far beyond linguistics. It is significant that Wormald has recently traced the origins of contemporary legal-historical studies directly to the work of Grimm and Kemble in the first half of the nineteenth century.[44]

Old English studies have moved from a period in which legal-historical problems were an intensive focus of philological work to a period in which such studies undoubtedly occupy the margins of the field and are rarely undertaken by specialists in literature. This study explores the consequences of this reconfiguration of the discipline for modern scholarship on *Beowulf*. The present study is also concerned with the uses to which *Beowulf* was put in attempts to reconstruct the system of Germanic law, and the problems inherent in such an approach. I am particularly interested in tracing the influence of the scholarly tradition known as the *historische Rechtsschule* (founded by figures such as Grimm and Wilhelm Eduard Wilda in the early nineteenth century) on the textual criticism and interpretation of *Beowulf*. The poem became an integral part of the scholarly

---

[44] See Wormald, *Making of English Law*, pp. 4-24.

effort to reconstruct Germanic legal institutions in 1828, when Grimm's *Deutsche Rechtsalterthümer* made extensive use of its contents to support his claim that Germanic law had been preserved by means of oral formulas much like those of Old English verse. Though Grimm's *Rechtsalterthümer* is now largely forgotten, throughout the nineteenth century it was seen by literary scholars and legal historians alike as a crucial text for the study of Germanic legal antiquities. Klaeber alludes to the *Rechtsalterthümer* almost as often as Grimm's more famous *Deutsche Mythologie,* yet no study has examined how the former influenced the assumptions of Klaeber and his contemporaries.

The effects of Grimm's *Rechtsalterthümer* on the critical heritage of *Beowulf* are examined in Chapter 1. In this text Grimm argued repeatedly that *Beowulf* contained traces of Common Germanic legal formulas, and even suggested emending the text to make more obvious the resemblance of these formulas to those of later, more explicitly legal texts. Some of these emendations survived into late nineteenth-century editions of the poem, while the belief that *Beowulf* preserves the remains of Germanic legal formulas frequently influences the textual criticism of Klaeber's edition.

Chapter 2 examines arguments from Grimm's *Rechtsalterthümer* that did not adduce evidence from *Beowulf* but nonetheless had lasting effects on the interpretation of the poem. Particularly important in the development of *Beowulf* criticism was Grimm's contention that *Gesammteigenthum* or "communal ownership" was a central feature of archaic Germanic law. In England, Grimm's arguments for the antiquity of *Gesammteigenthum* were received enthusiastically, for here a parallel was imagined with the English rights of common, which had been rendered obsolescent by the parliamentary enclosure movements of the eighteenth century. By the middle of the nineteenth century the loss of common rights was routinely lamented by Whig intellectuals, and ultimately incorporated into an existing political mythology in which pre-Conquest England was held to have been especially egalitarian and democratic.[45] Speculations about the collectivistic nature of Germanic landholding were introduced into *Beowulf* scholarship by Kemble. Inspired by arguments about *folcland* in John Allen's contemporaneous *Royal Prerogative in England* (1830), Kemble argued that *folcland* and hence the difficult term *folcscaru* (as it appears in *Beowulf* l. 73) designated land that was owned communally and thus inalienable by the king. Kemble's interpretation survives into Klaeber's unattributed gloss of *folcscaru* as "public land" which has remained standard to the present.

Later scholarship in the tradition of Grimm's *Rechtsalterthümer* continued to affect *Beowulf* scholarship significantly. The second half of this study is concerned primarily with the influence of post-Grimm legal-historical studies on the editing and interpretation of *Beowulf*. Chapter 3 examines a claim made in Wilda's *Strafrecht der Germanen* (1842) that vengeance was a sacred duty of the Germanic-speaking peoples. Statements such as these unduly influenced the interpretation of difficult passages in *Beowulf*, particularly the numerous textual cruces of the "Finn Episode." As Wilda's *Strafrecht* was a foundational text in the study of legal history, his arguments eventually found their way into literary studies of *Beowulf* and engendered an exaggerated emphasis on the duty of vengeance that has left us with a distorted picture of the Finn Episode's legal situation. For decades knowledge of the bloodfeud has been the principal tool by which scholarship has attempted to understand the Finn Episode. I argue that such an approach was necessitated solely by the dominant preoccupations of Germanist scholarship, and that there is no evidence within the text that the events described in the Finn Episode can be usefully discussed as feuding behavior.

Chapter 4 begins with a discussion of Heinrich Brunner's use of the Hrethel digression in a famous paper of 1890 as proof of his claim that accidental homicide had once been indistinguish-

---

[45] See Richard T. Vann, "The Free Anglo-Saxons: A Historical Myth," *Journal of the History of Ideas* 19 (1958), pp. 259-72.

able from deliberate homicide. Brunner's arguments, entering literary scholarship through Francis Gummere's *Germanic Origins* (1892), led generations of scholars to insist that Hæthcyn's accidental slaying of his brother Herebeald was punishable by death. Brunner's conclusions depended on methodologies that most contemporary legal historians consider outmoded, yet their influence on *Beowulf* scholarship persists. No contemporary discussions of the Hrethel digression disagree with Brunner's claim that Germanic law recognized no distinction between accidental and deliberate wrongs. This chapter discusses the wealth of evidence against this claim, and presents a reading of the Hrethel episode that is consonant with the major statements of Germanic legislation on the nature of accident.

As the following chapters will establish, attempts to use *Beowulf* as a source of evidence for lost or obsolescent institutions such as the right of common—indeed, the tendency of scholarship to reimagine the poem as a treasure-trove of Germanic antiquities—began as a response to the dearth of written evidence available to scholars who aimed to reconstruct archaic legal systems. That legal historians like Kemble, Grimm and Brunner could string together such chronologically and geographically disparate evidence reflects the extraordinary faith of these scholars in both the immutable nature of custom and the unity of social and institutional life among Germanic-speaking populations.[46] Indeed, a number of our most basic assumptions about the institutional background of *Beowulf* ultimately may reveal as much about the cultural history of nineteenth-century Germany and England as they do about the poem itself.

---

[46] This belief in the unchanging nature of customary law among illiterate populations that was so characteristic of scholarship in the nineteenth century was decisively repudiated by M. T. Clanchy's important article "Remembering the Past and the Good Old Law," *History* 55 (1970), pp. 165-76. The essay attempts to bring the study of early English law into agreement with the conclusions of anthropological studies more recent than those that influenced Maitland and his contemporaries.

# I

## JAKOB GRIMM, LEGAL FORMALISM
## AND THE EDITING OF *Beowulf*

UNTIL THE EARLY TWENTIETH CENTURY, *Beowulf* scholarship
was largely dominated by the view that the poem was an
amalgam of independent and sometimes highly archaic com-
positions. As T. A. Shippey observes, this assumption, known as
the *Liedertheorie*, was ultimately abandoned on both philological and critical grounds: Sievers's analyses found no metrical
variation of the sort that would be expected from a composite
poem, while the ascendancy of formalist literary criticism made
any approaches that suggested the poem's disunity less appeal-
ing.[1] Given the sweeping rejection of *Liedertheorie* methods in
contemporary Old English studies, it is surprising to observe
the unabated influence of an important if largely ignored sub-
category of *Liedertheorie* scholarship on the editing of *Beowulf*.
I refer to the suggestion made first in Jakob Grimm's *Deutsche
Rechtsalterthümer* (1828) that *Beowulf* occasionally preserves Germanic legal formulas, i.e., formalized speeches and phrases
that once were recited during legal proceedings. Eric Gerald
Stanley remains the only contemporary scholar to comment on

---

[1] The excesses of *Liedertheorie* scholarship are most apparent in Karl
Müllenhoff's famous article of 1869, which rejects all but 1,788 lines of
*Beowulf* as interpolations and attributes the poem to six different authors.
See Müllenhoff, "Die Innere Geschichte des Beowulfs," *Zeitschrift für
deutsches Altertum und deutsche Literatur* 14 (1869), pp. 193–244. A superb
overview of *Liedertheorie* scholarship remains that of Thomas Shippey,
"Structure and Unity," in Bjork and Niles, eds., *A Beowulf Handbook*, pp.
149–74.

Grimm's use of Germanic legal formulas as a means of elucidating passages from *Beowulf*.[2] But Stanley's account is for the most part descriptive, and does not attempt to evaluate the effects of Grimm's ideas on later scholarship.

Grimm's *Deutsche Rechtsalterthümer* and its comments on *Beowulf* cannot be ignored by those interested in how the modern text of the poem began its evolution in the early nineteenth century. Though now as neglected as his *Deutsche Grammatik* is celebrated, the *Rechtsalterthümer* dominated research into the social history of the Germanic peoples for well over a century, and its conclusions had lasting effects on literary as well as historical scholarship. In the notes to his edition of *Beowulf*, Klaeber alludes to the *Rechtsalterthümer* almost as often as he mentions Grimm's better-known *Deutsche Mythologie*.[3] Yet references to the *Rechtsalterthümer* are scarce in contemporary Old English scholarship. Any mention of the text is wholly omitted even from the recent *Beowulf Handbook*, most likely because the *Rechtsalterthümer* was never translated for English audiences as was the *Mythologie*.[4] As the following chapter will demonstrate, modern editors have defended a number of emendations—some of them quite drastic—which have their origins solely in the attempts of Grimm and his followers to recover the Germanic legal formulas allegedly underlying various passages within the poem. Before dealing with the emendations themselves, however, it

---

[2] E. G. Stanley, "The Scholarly Recovery of the Significance of Anglo-Saxon Records in Prose and Verse: A New Bibliography," *ASE* 9 (1981), pp. 223-262 at p. 234; see also *idem*, "The Continental Contribution to the Study of Anglo-Saxon Writings Up To and Including That of the Grimms," in *Towards a History of English Studies in Europe: Proceedings of the Wildsteig-Symposium, April 30-May 3, 1982*, eds. Thomas Finkenstaedt and Gertrud Scholtes (Augsburg: Universität Augsburg, 1983), pp. 9-39 at p. 22.

[3] See Klaeber, ed., *Beowulf*, pp. 192, 212, 213, 222.

[4] A sound overview of the *Rechtsalterthümer* in English can be found in Dobozy, "The Brothers Grimm," pp. 103-104.

will be necessary to sketch briefly the network of scholarly assumptions that once made them seem plausible to nineteenth-century editors of *Beowulf*. Grimm's *Rechtsalterthümer* began as a response to the claim made famous by Friedrich Carl von Savigny (a teacher and correspondent of Grimm's) that law is above all a reflection of the *Volksgeist,* and that for this reason legislators should resist the temptations of the codification movement then ascendant in France and instead encourage the preservation of Germany's native tradition of Roman law.[5]

Grimm assented to Savigny's belief that law was an element of culture, an expression of the peculiar habits and manners of discrete populations. But Grimm rejected the argument that Roman law was a trustworthy custodian of the German *Volksgeist,* since in his view the twelfth-century rediscovery of Justinian's *Digest* in Western Europe caused the widespread abandonment of Germanic institutions not substantially different from those described by Tacitus.[6] It was these institutions that the *Rechtsalterthümer* aimed to recover. Indeed, the tensions underlying early Germanic legal history were not unlike those that animated Germanic philology, since both aimed to supplant with their own languages and institutions the more prestigious literary language and legal monuments of Rome.

---

[5] One of Savigny's most celebrated contributions to nineteenth-century legal thought is his polemic "Vom Beruf unserer Zeit für Gesetzgebung und Rechtswissenschaft," in *Thibaut und Savigny,* ed. H. Hattenhauer (Munich: Vahlen, 1973), pp. 95-192. James Q. Whitman's *Legacy of Roman Law in the German Romantic Era* (Princeton: Princeton Univ. Press, 1990) is an excellent survey of the political environment of Savigny's career. His eloquent attack on the codification movement stimulated similar movements to privilege customary and popular institutions as far away as Catalonia: see Stephen Jacobson, "Law and Nationalism in Nineteenth-Century Europe: The Case of Catalonia in Comparative Perspective," *Law and History Review* 20 (2002), pp. 307-47.

[6] See Schmidt-Wiegand, "Das sinnliche Element des Rechts," pp. 7-8.

Such an undertaking required methodological innovations modeled on those of comparative philology, since Germanic legislation was inherently somewhat disappointing when compared with the great monuments of Roman law such as the *Digest*. With the exception of codes such as *Grágás* and the Norwegian Gulathing Law, most legislation in a Germanic language or context consisted largely of lists of tariffs, and few explanations of the abstract principles that stood behind them. Perhaps worst of all, there was little about pre-Reception law that was purely Germanic. No examples of Germanic legislation pre-date the conversion to Christianity, and so all result in some way from the fusion of Roman-Christian and Germanic cultures.[7]

Patrick Wormald has recently called attention to the fact that the major legal-historical publications of Grimm and his followers all took the form of glossaries and concordances. Wormald's explanation adduces the familiar notion of the *Volksgeist*, arguing that these texts assume law to be "a system inherent in society's soul, to bring out which it sufficed to supply an exhaustive set of references."[8] Stanley's observations on the same phenomenon suggest that the predilection of early legal historians for producing massive glossaries and concordances reflects the inevitably lexicographical bent of legal-historical scholarship in the nineteenth century.[9] Both explanations are certainly valid, but Grimm's own comments indicate a third basis for legal historians' drive to produce glossaries and concordances: specialized

---

[7] Richardson and Sayles contend that Æthelberht's code may have existed prior to St. Augustine's mission, but their arguments seem not to have gained widespread acceptance. See H. G. Richardson and G. O. Sayles, *Law and Legislation from Æthelberht to Magna Carta* (Edinburgh: Univ. of Edinburgh Press, 1966), pp. 1-12; 157-69.

[8] Patrick Wormald, *Making of English Law*, p. 23. Wormald refers here to the *Sachglossar* (vol. II) of Felix Liebermann's *Gesetze der Angelsachsen*.

[9] Stanley, "The Scholarly Recovery of the Significance of Anglo-Saxon Records," p. 233.

legal terms and frozen phrases were likely vestiges of the preliterate phase of legislation. Discussing the befuddled handling of Germanic legal terms in Frankish Latin legislation, Grimm states that his intent is not to explicate the terms but to demonstrate

> . . . daß sie nicht bloß dunkle wörter sind, sondern unserer alten rechtsterminologie angehören. Das wird sich auch aus ihrer einzelnen übereinstimmung unter einander in den verschiednen gesetzen und noch mehr mit den in der muttersprache abgefaßten angelsächs. und friesischen ergeben. Eine treffende bestätigung gewährt das altnordische recht, das, obgleich gar keine lat. redaction zur hervorhebung solcher ausdrücke nöthigte, sie mit den formeln *þat heitir, þat kalla,* die jenem quod dicitur, quod dicunt identisch sind, aufstellt.[10]

> . . . that they are not simply obscure words, but belong to our ancient legal language. This is proven by their individual correspondence with one another in the various legal codes and furthermore with those codes that are assembled in the native language such as those of the Anglo-Saxons and Frisians. A striking confirmation is offered by Old Norse law, which, although it required no Latin redaction to point out these terms, introduces them with formulaic expressions such as *þat heitir, þat kalla,* which are identical to expressions [from Frankish legislation] such as "quod dicitur," "quod dicunt."

Legislative memorials were useful in so far as they allowed Grimm to recover the varieties of Germanic lawmaking that had preceded the conversion of most Germanic-speaking peoples to Christianity and the subsequent introduction of Roman law. Accordingly, Grimm's *Deutsche Rechtsalterthümer* was concerned primarily with units of discourse (in this case, legal terms and phrases) whose presence in legislative texts betrayed their de-

---

[10] Grimm, *Deutsche Rechtsalterthümer,* p. 3.

pendence on preliterate modes of lawmaking that could be traced to pre-Christian antiquity. In addition to the technical legal terms of Germanic law, the residue of oral lawmaking was, according to Grimm, also apparent in the use of poetic formulas in Germanic legislative and diplomatic texts. In 1816, Grimm had argued that all Germanic legislation originally assumed some sort of poetic form: "Indeed it seems to me doubtless that in earliest antiquity our laws, no differently from legends and narratives, were likely assembled in verse."[11]

Expressions from the fourteenth-century *Sachsenspiegel* such as "Eigen und Erbe" and "Schuld und Schaden" permit us to hear, according to Grimm, "the ancient metrical mode still reverberate."[12] The presence of poetic features in legal texts was evidence for the archaism not of the texts, but of the expressions appearing within them. This was an important distinction, since the most obviously poetic legislation of the Germanic-speaking peoples—the *Sachsenspiegel* and the Frisian laws—were also the latest. By developing rudimentary criteria of oral composition to reveal the abiding influence of preliterate lawmaking, Grimm turned one of the shortcomings of Germanic law into its principal claim to legitimacy as a field of professional study. Because they were preserved orally, Germanic legal institutions offered a picture of the German *Volksgeist* more authentic, more popular and more archaic than the tradition of Roman law championed by Savigny, which was the exclusive province of an academic elite.[13]

---

[11] "Es liegt mir nämlich außer zweifel, daß unsere gesetze im frühsten alterthum wirklich, nicht anders wie sagen und geschichten, metrisch in lieder gebunden waren." Jakob Grimm, "Von der Poesie im Recht," *Zeitschrift für geschichtliche Rechtswissenschaft* 2 (1816), pp. 25-99 at p. 42.

[12] ". . . die alte metrische weise noch nachklingen." Grimm, "Von der Poesie im Recht," p. 43.

[13] See Grimm, "Von der Poesie im Recht," p. 30: "[K]einem dichter gehörte das lied; wer es sang wuste es blosz fertiger und treurer zu singen; eben so wenig gieng das ansehen des gesetzes aus von dem

*Jakob Grimm, Legal Formalism and the Editing of* Beowulf

Because all of the Germanic languages seemed to preserve the same inventory of legal terms and phrases, Grimm contended that all speakers of the Germanic languages inherited an ancient and culturally homogenous system of legal norms:

> Diese rechtsweisungen durch den mund des landvolks machen eine höchst eigenthümliche erscheinung in unserer alten ver- faßung, wie sie sich bei keinem andern volk wiederholt, und sind ein herrliches zeugnis der freien und edlen art unseres eingebornen rechts. Neu, beweglich und sich stets verjüngend in ihrer äußeren gestalt enthalten sie lauter hergekommene alte rechtsgebräuche und darunter solche, die längst keine an- wendung mehr litten, die aber vom gemeinen mann gläubig und in ehrfurchtsvoller scheu vernommen wurden. Sie können durch die lange fortpflanzung entstellt und vergröbert sein, un- echt und falsch sind sie nie. Ihre übereinstimmung unterein-

richter, der kein neues finden durfte; sondern die sänger verwalteten das gut der lieder, die urtheiler verweseten amt und dienst der rechte." Rudolf Huebner endorses Grimm's comparison of ancient Germanic law with popular ballads, and his *History of Germanic Private Law* (trans. Francis S. Philbrick, Continental Legal History Series, 4 [Boston: Little, Brown and Co., 1918], p. 9) contains the following translation of the passage: "[T]he song belonged to no poet; whoever sang it made it more true and more perfect in the singing; just as little did the prestige of the law proceed from the judge, who could not make a new one; the minstrels were guardians of the common property of song, and the judgment finders were entrusted with the office and ministry of the laws." That Germanic law was essentially popular and egalitarian is a doctrine traceable directly to Grimm which survived well into the 20th century: Huebner (pp. 8-9) states that law "lived, like morality and faith, within the consciousness, or rather within the feelings, of the common man. There was no need yet for scholars who made out of its study an independent profession. Every free member of the community knew how to apply it to the legal transactions of everyday life, and took part, in the court, in its application."

ander und mit einzelnen zügen alter, ferner gesetze muß jedem beobachter auffallen, und weist allein schon in ein hohes alterthum zurück. Es ist geradezu unmöglich, daß die poetischen formeln und gebräuche, deren die weisthümer voll sind, in den jahrhunderten ihrer aufzeichnung entsprungen sein sollten.[14]

These legal adages, (preserved) in the mouths of peasants, make a highly characteristic appearance in our ancient constitution, which is not found among any other people, and are a magnificent testimony to the free and noble nature of our native law. Fresh, flexible and always self-rejuvenating, they contain the pure survivals of ancient legal usages, including in their outer form those that long ago ceased to have any further usage, but which the common man heard with belief and awe. Through their long propagation they might have been garbled or coarsened, but they are never false or inauthentic. Their correspondence with one another and with individual features of ancient and remote legislation must be conspicuous to every observer, and already points back to a remote antiquity. It is clearly impossible that the poetic formulas and usages with which the legal literature is replete should have originated in the centuries in which they were written down.

Grimm's arguments regarding the poetic origins of Germanic law were widely accepted in the era during which the first and second editions of Klaeber's *Beowulf* appeared. Karl von Amira's entry in the *Grundriss der germanischen Philologie* (1913)

---

[14] Grimm, *Deutsche Rechtsalterthümer*, p. ix. The belief that ancient customs and usages were best preserved among the rural poor was shared by Kemble, whose written comments to Grimm on his *Rechtsalterthümer* observe that "[t]o this day peasants sometimes bring their wives to market . . . [T]his is punishable by law, but yet not uncommon, and must I think have its origin in some old customary Law." See Wiley, ed., *Correspondence*, p. 217 (no. 26). See also E. P. Thompson's unrivalled discussion of the practice in Thompson, *Customs in Common*, pp. 404–62.

shows the extent to which Grimm's assumptions had become articles of faith among Germanist legal historians when he refers to the "numerous oral formulas . . . which with other obsolete legal usages have withdrawn into popular custom."[15]

Recovering the vestiges of Germanic oral lawmaking remained a central concern of legal-historical scholarship. Von Amira classes the *Formeln* among specialized legal terms and proverbs, all three of which "we may refer to as oral, as they pass on the law by means of language, but not specifically in written form."[16] As late as 1932, Dorothy Bethurum offered qualified assent to Grimm's views in her discussion of Old English legislation: "The large number of legal formulas, many of them alliterative, many of them rhymed, which repeat themselves throughout the decrees of the Old English and Old Frisian laws, the *Sachsenspiegel,* and the Old Norse laws, lend some probability to the hypothesis of an original poetic form for the Germanic laws."[17] Bethurum goes on to claim the majority of alliterative formulas in Old English legislation as the remains of the pagan era.[18]

Grimm's arguments for the poetic origins of Germanic law made literary texts accessible as sources of evidence for legal

---

[15] ". . . mancherlei mündlichen Formeln . . . die mit anderen ehemaligen Rechtsgebräuchen sich in die Sitte des Volks zurückgezogen haben." Karl von Amira, *Grundriss des germanischen Rechts,* Grundriss der germanischen Philologie 5 (Strassburg: Verlag von Karl J. Trübner, 1913), p. 15.

[16] ". . . wir mündliche nennen können, weil sie zwar sprachlich, jedoch nicht wesentlich in Schriftform das Recht überliefern." See von Amira, *Grundriss,* p. 14.

[17] Dorothy Bethurum, "Stylistic Features of the Old English Laws," p. 266. Heinrich Brunner's belief in the poetic nature of archaic law was no less strong than that of his contemporaries: "Uralt ist die Sitte, Rechtssätze in allitterierende Formeln und in kurze Rechtssprichwörter zu fassen" ("The custom of presenting legal pronouncements in alliterating formulas and brief legal proverbs is ancient"). See Brunner, *Deutsche Rechtsgeschichte,* 2 vols. (Berlin: Verlag von Duncker & Humblot, 1906 repr. 1961), I, 153.

[18] Bethurum, "Stylistic Features of the Old English Laws," pp. 272-73.

historians—a move that was as much the result of practical necessity as theoretical exigency, given the small amount of Germanic legislation in the vernacular. It was the belief that all Germanic law had begun as poetry which permitted Grimm and his successors to begin mining literary texts such as *Beowulf* for passages that might augment the evidence available for arguments about continental and Scandinavian legislation. Where correspondences to Germanic legal principles were found in literary texts, their presence in metrical form was often held to be self-evident proof of their origins in the oral legal formulas of the prehistoric Germans, since all Germanic legislative statements had once assumed a metrical form.

A typical example of the legal formulas in which this sort of scholarship was especially interested is *Beowulf* l. 658, "Hafa nu ond geheald / husa selest" ("Have now and hold the best of houses"), a passage which is typical of some early Germanic verse and obviously corresponds to an alliterative formula familiar from weddings.

David Day has recently emphasized that the passage "sound[s] almost contractual, as if some legal transfer by hand is taking place," while Peter Tiersma's *Legal Language* (1999) cites the passage as an example of the kind of alliterative phrase "common in all the laws of the Germanic tribes."[19] Like Grimm (whom he cites as a central authority), Tiersma contends that the presence of alliteration in pre-Conquest English legislation reflects the fact that pleading in this era required "remembering exact verbal formulas."[20] Tiersma's views on this point appear somewhat old-fashioned given that contemporary legal-historical scholarship has for the most part become suspicious

[19] "Hands across the Hall: The Legalities of Beowulf's Fight with Grendel," *JEGP* 98 (1999), pp. 313-324 at p. 319; Peter J. Tiersma, *Legal Language* (Chicago: Univ. of Chicago Press, 1999), p. 14.

[20] Tiersma, *Legal Language*, p. 14.

of the *Rechtsschule* claim that litigants might lose cases because of verbal stumbles alone.[21]

### FORMULAS AS CRITERIA
### FOR TEXTUAL EMENDATION

The correspondence of the ancient and modern formula is in any case striking. But to what extent can entire passages from *Beowulf* be spoken of as legal formulas, and what are the interpretive implications of such claims? As I hope to demonstrate below, the common understanding of Wiglaf's speech reproaching the thanes who fled from Beowulf during his fight with the dragon shows traces of the once widespread interest in Germanic legal formulas. The passage appears in Klaeber's edition as follows:

> Nu sceal sincþego ond swyrdgifu,
> eall eðelwyn eowrum cynne,
> lufen alicgean; londrihtes mot
> þære mægburge monna æghwylc
> idel hweorfan, syððan æðelingas
> feorran gefricgean fleam eowerne,
> domleasan dæd. Deað bið sella
> eorla gehwylcum þonne edwitlif!

---

[21] The strict formalism of Germanic law was a central tenet of *Rechtsschule* scholarship, and was inseparable from assertions of its archaism: see e.g. Brunner, *Deutsche Rechtsgeschichte*, I, 254: "Nachmals finden wir, daß bei bestimmten Klagen besondere Formen zu beobachten waren, von welchen manche sicherlich in höchstes Altertum zurückreichen" ("Later we find that in certain cases particular forms were to be observed, of which many certainly go back to earliest antiquity"). For contemporary criticisms of this assumption see the Introduction to Wendy Davies and Paul Fouracre, eds., *The Settlement of Disputes in Early Medieval Europe* (Cambridge: Cambridge Univ. Press, 1986), p. 3.

Now shall cease for your kind all distribution of treasure and
swords, all the enjoyment of home and comfort. Each man of
your kindred must go without rights in land when nobles hear
from far off of your flight, your shameful deed. Death is better
for each earl than a life of disgrace!

In his *Rechtsalterthümer*, Grimm took more interest in ll. 2884-
2891 than in any other passage from *Beowulf*. To Grimm they were
proof of the supposedly Common Germanic rule that deserters
in battle were to be cut off from the society of other men and de-
nied the privileges ensured by folk law. In support he mentions
(as does Klaeber) chapter 6 of Tacitus's *Germania:* "Scutum rel-
iquisse praecipuum flagitium, nec aut sacris adesse aut concilium
inire ignominioso fas; multique superstites bellorum infamiam
laqueo finierunt" ("To have abandoned one's shield is the great-
est shame, nor is it permitted to such an ignominious man to be
present at religious rites or councils; many who have survived
battle have ended their infamy with a noose").[22] Also mentioned
is the legislation of Frotho as preserved in Saxo Grammaticus: "Si
quis in acie primus fugam capesseret, a communi jure alienus ex-
isteret" ("Should one be the first to take flight from the advance
of battle, let him be expelled from the law of the community").[23]
Grimm saw the latter's reference to expulsion from the *communi
iure* as synonymous with the loss of *londriht* by the doomed retainers in *Beowulf*, presumably because Old English *londriht* is cognate with Modern German *Landrecht*, "provincial law."

As Wiglaf's speech relates an ancient principle of Germanic
law, it is hardly surprising that Grimm cites the passage earlier in
his study as "an example of an archaic formula of banishment"
and places it among other formulas from Old Norse and Middle
High German legislation.[24] It was at this point that speculation

---

[22] Tacitus, *Germania*, p. 41.

[23] Quoted in Grimm, *Deutsche Rechtsalterthümer*, p. 731.

[24] ". . . beispiel einer alten verbannungsformel." Grimm, *Deutsche
Rechtsalterthümer*, p. 42.

about the supposedly juridical origins of poetic passages began to have lasting consequences for the edited text of *Beowulf.* Grimm believed the *Beowulf* poet preserved the formula imperfectly, and so it became necessary to make the correspondence more obvious between the written text and the oral formula that had necessarily preceded it. On these grounds, Grimm suggested *lufen* (defined by Klaeber as "joy," "comfort," or "homestead," and related etymologically to *lufian*) might be a corruption of *leofen,* "sustenance:" "I take *lufen* to be *leofen,* 'victus,' and therefore *wyn and lufen* corresponds to our legal formula *wonne und weide,* 'joy and pasture'."[25] The proposed emendation is characteristic of the interpretive strategies underlying early Germanist scholarship, and calls to mind the objections of scholars such as Rask to Grimm's organization of all Germanic languages under the supposedly neutral label *deutsch.*[26] It is significant, for example, that the hypothetical original form of the passage in question is disclosed only by its resemblance to "our legal formula" (*unserer rechtsformel*); a formula which, though undoubtedly later than the passage in *Beowulf,* should nonetheless serve as the basis of its emendation given that Grimm etymologically relates Old English *wyn* ("joy") to Modern German *Wonne.*[27] Perhaps the most troubling aspect of Grimm's proposed emendation (insignificant as it is to our understanding of the poem as a whole) is his willingness to assume the existence of an independent Old English legal formula "wyn and leofen" solely because a similar collocation is attested in Modern German. One

[25] "*[L]ufen* nehme ich für *leofen* 'victus,' und dann entspricht *wyn and lufen* ganz unserer rechtsformel *wonne und weide.*" Grimm, *Deutsche Rechtsalterthümer,* p. 731 n. 2.

[26] A sound overview of this controversy appears in Hans Frede Nielsen, "Jacob Grimm and the 'German' Dialects," in Antonsen, ed., *The Grimm Brothers and the Germanic Past,* pp. 25-32.

[27] See the entry for "Wonne" in Hermann Paul, *Deutsches Wörterbuch: Bedeutungsgeschichte und Aufbau unseres Wortschatzes,* rev. ed. by Helmut Henne *et al.* (Tübingen: Max Niemeyer, 2002).

should reasonably expect truly formulaic expressions to appear with some frequency, as do the familiar collocations "hafa ond geheald" ("have and hold") and "wordum ond weorcum" ("with words and with deeds"). Yet the only collocation of "wyn and lufen" to be found in Old English occurs in ll. 2885-6 of *Beowulf*. Between these two words falls an abundance of material that seems not to have sustained Grimm's interest once he heard in this portion of the poem a dim echo of a familiar legal adage.

Grimm likewise accepted without comment the emendation of MS *hu* to *nu* suggested originally by his friend and student, J. M. Kemble, who was simultaneously preparing the first modern edition of *Beowulf*. However slight Kemble's emendation might be, it is clear that the alteration of MS *hu* ("how") to *nu* ("now") changes the nature of the utterance significantly. Though the change does indeed improve the progress of the narrative, it also has served over the years to reinforce the impression originated by Grimm that Wiglaf's speech is a Germanic legal formula rather than a lament or exclamation of a type widely attested in Old English verse.

In 1859 Karl Bouterwek defended the emendations suggested by Kemble and Grimm on the grounds that the passage is really a legal formula adapted to the poem: "[T]he slight emendations of the manuscript . . . facilitate the understanding of this perhaps poetically (but nonetheless) altered formula."[28]

The change of *lufen* to *leofen* was retained as late as Moritz Trautmann's edition of 1904. In the following year, Friedrich Holthausen suggested that the alteration of MS *hu* to *nu* might

[28] "[D]ie kleinen veränderungen gegen die hs., *nû* statt *hû* (auch Th.), *lufen â licgean* statt des *lufena licgean* der hs. . . . erleichtern das verständniss dieser vielleicht dichterisch dennoch abgeänderten formel." See Karl W. Bouterwek, "Zur Kritik des Beowulfliedes," *Zeitschrift für deutsches Altertum* 11 (1859), pp. 59-113 at p. 108.

have been unnecessary, for the passage may well be an ex-
clamatory clause of the type found in *Wanderer* l. 95: "Hu seo
þrag gewat, // genap under niht-helm / swa heo na wære!"
("How the time passed, darkened under the cover of night,
as if it never were!").[29] The Chambers/Wyatt edition repeated
Holthausen's suggestion. Other examples of this usage of Old
English *hu* are certainly abundant.[30]

It is somewhat surprising to note the total unwillingness of
modern editors to accept the manuscript reading. Else von
Schaubert's recension of the Heyne-Schücking *Beowulf* says pe-
remptorily that Holthausen's and Chambers's arguments for the
restoration of MS *hu* simply "fall flat," a strangely vehement denunciation given the significant evidence in their favor.[31] Hoops
likewise dismisses Chambers's suggestion as "improbable" and
offers no further explanation.[32] At least Dobbie attempts to provide a substantial argument for retention of Kemble's emenda-

---

[29] The passage from *The Wanderer* is cited from *Eight Old English Poems*,
eds. John C. Pope and R. D. Fulk (New York: Norton, 2001).

[30] *Andreas* ll. 63-64: "Hu me elþeodige / inwitwrasne // searonet seowað!";
*Christ* ll. 130-33: "Eala gasta god, / hu þu gleawlice // mid noman ryhte
/ nemned wære // Emmanuhel, / swa hit engel gecwæð // ærest on
Ebresc!". *Christ* ll. 216-21: "Eala þu soða / ond þu sibsuma // ealra
cyninga cyning, / Crist ælmihtig, // hu þu ær wære / eallum geworden
// worolde þrymmum / mid þine wuldorfæder // cild acenned / þurh
his creaft ond meaht!"; *Christ* l. 1459: "Hu þær wæs unefen racu / unc
gemæne!" Citations from *Christ* are drawn from *The Exeter Book*, ASPR
III, eds. George Philip Krapp and Elliott Van Kirk Dobbie (New York:
Columbia Univ. Press, 1936); *Andreas* is cited from *The Vercelli Book*,
ASPR II, ed. George Philip Krapp (New York: Columbia Univ. Press,
1932). All of the passages were first collected in Dobbie, ed., *Beowulf*,
p. 262 n. 2884.

[31] Else von Schaubert, *Heyne-Schücking's Beowulf*, 16th ed. (Paderborn:
Verlag Ferdinand Schöningh, 1946), p. 108 n. 2884.

[32] Johannes Hoops, *Kommentar zum Beowulf* (Heidelberg: Carl Winters
Verlag, 1932), p. 301 n. 2884.

tion when he asserts that ll. 2884-2890a constitute a "continued prophecy."[33] Most contemporary editors reproduce the Kemble/Grimm emendation without any significant comment. What is most surprising about the comments mentioned above is the way in which support for retention of the manuscript reading does not fall along the expected party lines of editorial conservatism and liberalism. Though Chambers was a vigorous defender of conservative editing, Holthausen sought a middle road that would avoid the extremes of Trautmann's edition. Moreover, it was von Schaubert's edition, which Fulk has called a "conservative standard" among twentienth-century editions of *Beowulf,* whose attitude toward the Holthausen/Chambers proposal was the most dismissive of all the modern editors to comment on the passage.[34]

What is of most interest in the dispute described above are the views of the passage, and ultimately the poem, which the respective editors brought to the discussion, views which attest to the survival of very old ideas. We are accustomed to thinking of nineteenth-century textual scholarship on *Beowulf* as dominated by a desire either to recover the poem's lost archetype, or, as in the case of Müllenhoff and Levin Schücking, to recover the lost Germanic folk poems of which *Beowulf* is an amalgamation. But Grimm's and Bouterwek's observations suggest that nineteenth-century formula hunters might also pursue material that was not explicitly poetic in nature, and argue for reconstructive editing of the poem on the basis of their discoveries. Unlike even the most zealous *Liedertheorie* protagonists, scholars such as Grimm and Bouterwek were able to privilege recovery of *Beowulf*'s legal formulas over recovery of the original features of the poem. That

---

[33] Dobbie, *Beowulf and Judith,* p. 262 n. 2884. Dobbie's use of the term "prophecy" may reflect the influence of Gummere's *Germanic Origins* (New York: Scribner's, 1892), which refers to Wiglaf's speech as a "prophecy of denunciation" (p. 266).

[34] Fulk, "Textual Criticism," in Bjork and Niles, eds., *A Beowulf Handbook,* p. 36.

the recovery of legal formulas was sometimes felt to be a more important goal than the recovery of the poem is not surprising, since the formulas were necessarily older, and hence more precious to scholarship according to what were then the prevailing assumptions, than the archetype of *Beowulf* itself. Attitudes not unlike those of Grimm and Bouterwek survive into contemporary *Beowulf* scholarship—not, I suspect, because of continued interest in Jakob Grimm or *Rechtsschule* methods, but because the scholarly tradition inaugurated by Grimm established the dominant paradigm for all subsequent study of *Beowulf*'s social setting. That these attitudes endure becomes clear when we examine the choice of words used by some scholars to describe the genre of Wiglaf's speech to Beowulf's retainers. Hoops referred to the passage as a "Bestrafung von Gefolgsleuten," a description that suggests Wiglaf is passing a kind of sentence on the warriors.[35] Klaeber in turn refers to the passage as "the announcement of punishment to the faithless retainers," a description that is probably echoed by John M. Hill when he refers to ll. 2884-91 as Wiglaf's "edict against the cowards."[36] All of these scholars suggest that Wiglaf's speech is some kind of formal legal pronouncement. That Grimm's view of this passage has endured so long in Old English scholarship is less a demonstration of its merits than of the longevity Klaeber's *Beowulf* gave to early nineteenth-century ideas that might otherwise have been forgotten.

## ANATHEMAS, CHARTERS AND CURSED GOLD

We can see how the legacy of Grimm and Bouterwek resurfaces elsewhere in *Beowulf* scholarship by examining some of the major solutions to what is probably the best-known crux of the poem, that of ll. 3074-75. The number of conjectures offered for this passage is vast, and a complete review of them here would

[35] Hoops, *Kommentar,* p. 301 n. 2884.

[36] Klaeber, ed., *Beowulf,* p. 222 n. 2884; John M. Hill, *The Cultural World in* Beowulf (Toronto: Univ. of Toronto Press, 1995), p. 136.

not be helpful. A glance at the solutions arrived at by some of the major editors gives a fair sense of the most important proposals over the last century:[37]

> *MS (Zupitza):*
> næshe goldhwæte gearwor hæfde agendes est ær ge sceawod
>
> *Wyatt-Chambers:*
> næs he gold-hwæte   gearwor hæfde
> Agendes est   ær gesceawod
>
> *Heyne-Schücking (von Schaubert):*
> næs he gold-hwæte  gearwor hæfde
> agendes est   ær gesceawod
>
> *Klaeber:*
> næ*fne* goldhwæte   gearwor hæfde
> Agendes est   ær gesceawod

The problems inhere mainly in the interpretation of the pronoun in l. 3074: does *he* refer to Beowulf or to *se secg* ("the man") of l. 3071? Also troublesome are the obscure compound *goldhwæte* and the ambiguous referent of *agendes*: does the latter refer to the original possessor(s) of the treasure, to the dragon, or to God as in *Exodus* l. 295?

---

[37] Here I have refrained from my usual practice of translating Old English because of the exceptional difficulties of this passage: its possible meanings should be made clear in the subsequent discussion. The most recent discussion of this passage contends that "lines 3074-75 punctuate Beowulf's movement into knowing and assert that he arrives at the highest level of *sapientia,* insofar as he sees and understands as never before how God's design includes and incorporates him." See Jonathan Myerov, "Lines 3074-3075 in *Beowulf:* Movement into Knowing," *Anglia* 118 (2000), pp. 531-55 at p. 532.

A solution has been sought in abandoning the possibility that *næs* is a negative contraction (*ne wæs* > *næs*) and taking it instead to be an error for the conjunction *næfne* ("unless"). An eloquent if problematic defense of the emendation to *næfne* was offered by W. W. Lawrence, who argued in 1918 that the passage resembles ll. 3051–57, another description of the curse placed on the gold:

> þone wæs þæt yrfe    eacencræftig
> iumonna gold    galdre bewunden
> þæt ðæm hringsele    hrinan ne moste
> gumena ænig,    nefne God sylfa,
> sigora Soðcyning    sealde þam ðe he wolde
> —he is manna gehyld—    hord openian
> efne swa hwylcum manna,    swa him gemet ðuhte.

> Then was that immense heritage, the gold of the men of old, encircled with a spell, so that no man could reach the ring-hall unless God himself, the true king of victories, granted to him that he desired—he is the protection of men—to open the hoard; even to him whom he [God] thought meet.

Lawrence's arguments in support of this parallelism begin from the assumption that Beowulf's death reflects the narrative in its pre-Christian state. The references to God and his ability to avert the curse are necessitated by the poet's unwillingness to acknowledge the power of pagan curses. They indicate a failure to synthesize pagan and Christian beliefs:

> The fact that the very pious hero falls a victim to the curse is one of the inconsistencies into which the poet was led in a re-telling of the old pagan tale with a new motivation. The Christian God was superior to spells, and the Christian hero was the one who ought to have been saved by the Christian God, on account of his piety; but the story made him die, and so there

was nothing for the poet to do but to leave to the old charms and the dragon power enough to kill him off.[38]

Lawrence's solution resorts to what was then the conventional remedy of attributing moments of awkwardness in the poem to a meddlesome cleric—in this case, a cleric who added a disclaimer disparaging the efficacy of pagan curses.[39] A significant weakness of his proposal, as Klaeber observed later, is its failure to consider how such an error might have arisen. While he considered the emendation to *næfne* an advance over earlier readings, Klaeber emphasized Sievers's earlier suggestion that the entirety of MS *næshe* was a plausible error for *næfne*: to substitute freely *næfne* for *næs* was too convenient. The emendation adopted by Klaeber is as follows: "*næfne goldhwæte* (or *–hwæt*[n]*e*) *gearwor hæfde / Agendes est ær gesceawod*, i.e., 'unless God's grace (or, kindness) had before (or, first) more readily (or, thoroughly) favored those (or, the one) eager for gold.'"[40]

Klaeber's emendation ultimately did little to obviate the problems of ll. 3074-75—something that probably was not lost on Klaeber himself, who concedes that the passage remains a "locus desperatus."[41] In addition to depending on a severe emendation, Klaeber's arguments assume an at least unusual definition of *gesceawod*, and improbable definitions for *goldhwæte* and *est*. His reading was soon taken to task by Hoops in 1932:

> [G]*oldhwæt* 3074 kann wohl nur "goldreich" heißen, wie schon Grein übersetzte, nicht "scharf auf Gold, goldgierig", wie es seit Thorpe von den meisten gedeutet wird. *hwæt* als

---

[38] W. W. Lawrence, "The Dragon and His Lair in *Beowulf*," *PMLA* n.s. 26 (1918), pp. 547-583 at p. 563.

[39] The proposal that the passage was interpolated was first made in Eduard Sievers, "Beowulf 3066ff.," *Beiträge zur Geschichte der deutschen Sprache und Literatur* 55 (1931), p. 376.

[40] Klaeber, ed., *Beowulf*, p. 227.

[41] Klaeber, ed., *Beowulf*, p. 227.

zweites Glied von adjektivischen Kompositis bedeutet "stark an, reich an, tüchtig in" der Sache oder Eigenschaft, die das erste Kompositionsglied ausdrückt: *bled-hwæt* "fruchtreich", *fyrd-hwæt* "heerestüchtig, kriegstüchtig", *mod-hwæt*, "mutig." Auch *dæd-hwæt* heißt wohl "tatkräftig", nicht "tatendurstig"; *guð-hwæt* "kampftüchtig", nicht "kampflustig". Wenn aber *gold-hwæt* "goldreich" bedeutet, ist es offenbar mit *est* zu verbinden.[42]

*goldhwæt* 3074 can surely only mean "rich in gold," as Grein already translated it, not "eager for gold," "gold-greedy," as it has been interpreted since Thorpe by the majority of editors. *hwæt* as the second element of an adjectival compound means "strong in," "rich in," "skilled in" the matter or attribute expressed by the first element of the compound: *bled-hwæt* "rich in fruit," *fyrd-hwæt*, "skilled in military affairs, skilled in battle," *mod-hwæt*, "brave." Also *dæd-hwæt* most likely means "strong in deeds," not "thirsty for action"; *guð-hwæt* "skilled in battle," not "battle-loving." But if *gold-hwæt* means "rich in gold," it clearly modifies *est*.

Hoops found every other assumption of Klaeber equally faulty. His assumption that *est* cannot mean as it does elsewhere in the poem "legacy" or "inheritance" unnecessarily excludes the possibility that *goldhwæte* is not an epithet for Beowulf but an adjective modifying *est*. The assumption that *agend* refers to God was likewise unattractive to Hoops.

It remained for Rudolf Imelmann to explore the implications of a possibility that all preceding scholarship had been unwilling to entertain. Should we assume *næs* to be not a negative contraction but a shortened form of *ne ealles*, "by no means" (as is the case in *Beowulf* l. 562 and l. 2262), we arrive at a reading of the line that requires no emendation, no eccentric definitions, and no awkward break with the preceding lines: "nor would he have beheld the owner's gold-abounding

[42] Hoops, *Kommentar*, p. 319.

legacy more fully."[43] The reading was accepted without qualification by Dobbie.[44] Though rejected by a number of editors, Klaeber's emendation abides through the medium of E. Talbot Donaldson's standard translation, which remains that of Klaeber in most respects. The dominance of Klaeber's edition in pedagogy and scholarship has likewise never abated. With such an impressive array of evidence against his proposal, it is certainly surprising that Klaeber did not think to abandon it in his final edition. Yet Klaeber found support for his reading in its apparent resemblance to the standard anathema of Anglo-Saxon charters and other ecclesiastical documents: "That the 'incantation' should end with a clause showing a way to avoid the threatened curse, is in line with a practice observed in Formulas of Excommunication. The same feature occurs at the end of Charters."[45] Klaeber's contention that the passage somehow resembles the anathema clause of charters was later supported by Kenneth Sisam, who went further in seeing the correspondence between the passage and charter language as proof of Sievers's old claim that the passage describing the curse is a Christian interpolation:

> Sievers's later work cannot safely be used by those who do not accept his premises; yet surely delicacy of ear or the instinct of genius had led him to the right solution here: that these five lines are an interpolation. It is the more likely because they have their parallel in formal dedications of property: they correspond to the usual clause in Anglo-Saxon charters which threatens anybody who breaks the disposition with damnation,

---

[43] See Rudolf Imelmann, "Beowulf 303ff. und 3074f.," *Englische Studien* 67 (1933), pp. 325-339; idem, "Beowulf 3074f.: Nachprüfung," *Englische Studien* 68 (1933), pp. 1-5.

[44] See Dobbie, ed., *Beowulf*, p. 274.

[45] Klaeber, ed., *Beowulf*, p. 227.

the companionship of Judas, of Ananias and Sapphira, or the like.[46]

All of these proposals are ultimately traceable to Bouterwek's much earlier assertion that the description of the curse is "a formula . . . which was recited during the burial of treasures."[47] On the question of whether the curse was pagan or Christian, oral or literate in nature, Bouterwek seems to have been unable to make up his mind, though he does adduce a passage from Kemble's *Codex Diplomaticus Ævi Saxonici*, mentioned so as to suggest the similarity between the passage describing the curse and the anathemas that conclude most Anglo-Saxon charters. Yet there is one important respect in which Bouterwek's and Sisam's discussions should be distinguished from Klaeber's: the former two assiduously avoid any discussion of the last problematic line of the curse.

Klaeber's suggestion that ll. 3074-75 echo the language of charters has to my knowledge never been disputed. Certainly there is nothing implausible about the suggestion that here *Beowulf* might share a common idiom with diplomatic texts. But can this supposed resemblance be deployed as a basis for emendation? If so, we should at least require that the resemblance be fairly explicit.

But Klaeber does not refer specifically to any charters or other documents, and one suspects that had he done so, the supposed affinity between the curse and anathema clauses would not have seemed quite as self-evident as his language suggests. Some typical examples of the anathema clauses from charters and excommunication formulas that offer a means of averting

[46] Kenneth Sisam, "Beowulf's Fight with the Dragon," *RES* n.s. 9 (1958), 128-140 at 130-31.

[47] ". . . eine formel . . . die bei vergrabung von schätzen ausgesprochen ward." Bouterwek, "Zur Kritik des Beowulfliedes," p. 109.

the penalties for meddling in the disposition of property are as follows:

*Oswold (32)*
Gief hwa . . . hit awendan wille, God adilgie his noman of lifes bocum, ⁊ habbe him gemæne wið hine on þam ytemestan dæge þisses lifes butan he to rihtere bote gecerre.

*Ælfweard (36)*
Se þe þis gehealde, gehealde hine God, ⁊ se ðe hit awende oððe gelytlige, gelitlige God his mede on þam toweardum life, butan he hit ær his ende þe deoppor gebete.

*Cambridge, Corpus Christi College 422 p. 16 (Liebermann V, p. 435):*
Et sicut extinguuntur iste lucerne, ita iaceant eorum anime in inferno cum diabolo et angelis eius; nisi resipiscant et ad emen-dacionem congruam ueniant.

*Cambridge, Corpus Christi College 303 p. 339 (Liebermann VII, p. 438):*
Đurhwunian hi awergoden fram þæs fotes tredele oð ufewearde þæs heafdes hnolle, buton hi selfa underþæncan ⁊ to dædbote cuman![48]

*Oswold:*
If someone . . . will alter it, may God blot out his name from the book of life, and may he have sorrow with him on the utmost day of this life unless he turns to better restitution;

---

[48] Charters are cited according to the numeration in Henry Sweet, *A Second Anglo-Saxon Reader. Archaic and Dialectal*, 2nd ed. rev. T. F. Hoad (Oxford: Clarendon, 1978). Parenthetical citations following excommunication formulas are according to the page numbers and numeration of Liebermann, *Gesetze*, I.

*Ælfweard:*
He who holds this, may God keep him, and [for] him who alters it or diminishes [it], may God diminish his reward in the life to come, unless he makes a more profound restitution before his end;

*CCCC 422:*
And as these lamps are extinguished, so may their souls fall into hell with the devil and his angels, unless they come to their senses and arrive at an appropriate restitution:

*CCCC 303:*
May they endure cursed from the step of the foot up to the inner part of the crown of the head, unless they themselves consider [their deed] and come to repentance!

Though a general resemblance between the anathema clauses and Klaeber's reconstructed line is conceivable, such a resemblance is hard to reconcile with the uniform requirement of anathema clauses that those who are excommunicated or who meddle in the disposition of charters must first seek amends with God before they can expect to avoid divine punishment. Klaeber's emendation establishes an escape clause in the curse, one which allows for the possibility that God might permit the violation of a solemn behest, a condition that is contrary to the most basic function of anathemas. While the resemblance posited by Klaeber is in many ways suggestive, it certainly does not offer any reliable grounds for emendation of the text.

## CONCLUSION

Had an early adherent to Grimm's legal-historical theories not seen in the curse a suggestion of early Germanic legal customs, perhaps the formidable powers of scholars like Klaeber and Sisam would never have been devoted to establishing the legal-historical pedigree of this passage. Their attempts to do so were clearly determined by the scholarly tradition within which they worked. This was a tradition that looked with some disdain (not always without justification) on the work of the two scribes of the *Beowulf* manuscript, and that had held, ever since the era of Grimm and Kemble, that *Beowulf* was often reducible to a series of disconnected formal utterances, usually poetic but, in the case of the examples discussed in this chapter, often legal. As has been demonstrated in the above discussion, solutions to textual cruces in the nineteenth century often depended upon one's talent for reconstructing passages independently of their context within the poem. The merest suggestion that passages from *Beowulf* echoed the cadences of the Germanic tradition of metrical lawmaking entitled scholars to adapt these passages freely to their imagined exemplars. All such emendations bolstered popular and scholarly belief in the ancient constitution of the Germanic-speaking peoples and augmented the wealth of material by which its institutions might be reconstructed.

# II

## "Public Land," Germanic Egalitarianism, and Nineteenth-century Philology

IN *Beowulf* WE ARE TOLD that, upon the completion of Heo-rot, King Hrothgar intended to distribute to young and old all that God had given him with two exceptions: he could not give the "folk-share" (*folcscare*) and the lives of men (*feorum gumena*).[1] This passage has vexed *Beowulf* scholarship since the beginning of modern textual editing in the nineteenth century. *Beowulf* l. 73 seems to have no parallels in Old English prose or verse, and a number of scholars have assumed the line to be defective.

Arguments for corrective emendation begin in 1889, with Richard Heinzel's proposal that the line should be changed (ungrammatically) to *bútú folcscare ond feorum gumena*, "both to his own people and to strangers."[2] As late as 1953, Norman Eliason proposed the less conjectural emendation of the line

[1] The entire passage from *Beowulf* is as follows: "Him on mod bearn, // þæt healreced / hatan wolde // medoærn micel / men gewyrcean // þon[n]e yldo bearn / æfre gefrunon, // ond þær on innan / eall gedælan // geongum ond ealdum, / swylc him God sealde // buton folcscare / ond feorum gumena" ("It began to run about it in his [Hrothgar's] mind that he would command men to construct a hall, a mead-hall greater than the children of men had ever heard of, and within it he would distribute to young and old all that God had given him except for the *folcscare* and the lives of men [ll. 67-73]").

[2] Richard Heinzel, "Moritz Heyne's *Beowulf. Mit ausführlichem Glossar herausgegeben* (fünfte Auflage)," *Anzeiger für deutsches Altertum und deutsche Literatur*, 15 (1889), p. 189.

to "buton folcscare ond feorm gumena" ("except for the folk-share and the food of men").[3] Eliason's argument is based largely on the supposition that no evidence exists for royal donations of land and men in Anglo-Saxon England.

In 1892 P. J. Cosijn made the more influential guess that line 73, since it apparently "stands alone" in the corpus of Old English prose and verse, might be a late interpolation. On its own, Cosijn maintained, the line was "absolutely incomprehensible," though he does speculate that it might be a "snide remark aimed at an Anglian ruler, who thinned out his army by allowing it to fight under the banners of another king, instead of in defense of his own land."[4] Cosijn's suggestion that line 73 is interpolated was taken up by Klaeber, resurfacing in the latter's claim that the line is one of seventeen "corrective additions."[5] Later Klaeber attempts to explain line 73 by reference to a passage from Tacitus, in which we are told that the continental *Germani* were not in the habit of granting unlimited powers to their kings.[6] While its assertion that Germanic kings did not have the power of capital punishment would seem to

[3] Norman Eliason, *"Beowulf* Notes," *Anglia* 71 (1953), pp. 438-55 at pp. 438-39. Though Eliason's arguments for emendation are the most cogent to date, they do seem essentially based on the view that *feorum gumena* does not make sense; I shall offer evidence that it does.

[4] See P. J. Cosijn, *Aanteekeningen op den* Béowulf, trans. as *Notes on Beowulf,* Leeds Texts and Monographs n.s. 12, eds. and trans. Rolf H. Bremmer Jr. *et al.* (Leeds: Univ. of Leeds, 1991), pp. 2-3.

[5] Klaeber, *Beowulf,* p. cvii.

[6] Klaeber, Beowulf, p. 270. See Tacitus, *Germania,* p. 43: "Reges ex nobilitate, duces ex virtute sumunt. nec regibus infinita aut libera potestas" ("They choose their kings on the ground of birth, their generals according to their courage. The power of their kings is not infinite or arbitrary"). Klaeber was probably drawing here on a University of Göttingen dissertation by Johannes Müller (*Das Kulturbild des Beowulfepos,* Studien zur englischen Philologie LIII [Halle: Max Niemeyer, 1914], p. 2); the latter had been the first to connect the passage in Tacitus with *Beowulf* l. 73 and took

parallel Hrothgar's inability (or refusal) to give "the lives of men," the example from Tacitus adduced by Klaeber says nothing about the powers of kings to donate land.

There is every reason to continue to believe, as editors have for some time, that *Beowulf* l. 73 is a reference to the royal donation of land. It is odd that Klaeber does not mention potential parallels that are geographically and chronologically closer to *Beowulf,* such as Bede's letter to Egbert.

Here Bede complains that lands in England have been donated too liberally to monasteries, leaving little for young soldiers and thus forcing the latter to go abroad in search of lands on which to establish themselves.[7] Indeed, the only genuinely peculiar thing about line 73 is that we should be told so pointedly that Hrothgar could not make the sort of donations of land that ostensibly were commonplace within and outside of the poem.[8]

their apparent similarity as evidence for the "astonishingly tenacious constancy of Germanic conditions" ("erstaunliche Beharrlichkeit der germanischen Verhältnisse"): quotation and translation are from E. G. Stanley, *Imagining the Anglo-Saxon Past* (Woodbridge: D. S. Brewer, 2000), p. 65.

[7] "For—what is indeed disgraceful to tell—those who are totally ignorant of the monastic life have received under their control so many places in the name of monasteries, as you yourself know better than I, that there is a complete lack of places where the sons of nobles or of veteran thegns can receive an estate; and thus, unoccupied and unmarried, though the time of puberty is over, they persist in no intention of continence, and on this account they either leave the country for which they ought to fight and go across the sea, or else with greater guilt and shamelessness they devote themselves to loose living and fornication, seeing they have no intention of chastity, and do not even abstain from virgins consecrated to God." The translation is given in Dorothy Whitelock, ed. and trans., *English Historical Documents vol. 1, c. 550-1042,* 2nd ed. (London: Eyre and Spottiswoode, 1979), pp. 735-45.

[8] For example, Hygelac rewards Beowulf handsomely for military service with a gift of land: see Klaeber, ed., *Beowulf* ll. 2194-97, 2490-93.

The collocation of land and men is certainly less mysterious than prior scholarship has assumed.[9] Though its ultimate relation to *Beowulf* l. 73 may remain obscure, there may be a poetic parallel in the Old English *Exodus*, when God grants power to Moses over the lives of his kin (*maga feorh*) and the lands (*onwist eðles*).[10] In its specific allusion to restraints on royal authority to donate land and men, *Beowulf* l. 73 is certainly not a passage which ever was in isolation. As Susan Reynolds notes, early medieval land grants almost never conveyed land alone, since the land "presumably had peasants on it."[11]

The practice of Germanic kings in Visigothic Spain, for example, may offer a suggestive parallel for the restraints on royal alienation of land and men in *Beowulf*. In the *Forum Judicum* we find some of the earliest written legal restraints against the power of Germanic kings to alienate land and possessions. These laws, promulgated first by King Reccaswinth in 652, require that all legitimate alienations of property by the king be made in writing and subjected to a process of conciliar review. What is curious about this passage, and perhaps relevant in some way to the situation in *Beowulf,* is the way in which this text makes particular mention of donations of slaves and land: "Similis quoque ordo *de terris, vineis, adque familiis* observetur, si sine scripture textum tantumodo coram testibus quelibet facta fuerit definitio" ("The rule shall similarly be observed concerning [donations] of land, vine-

---

[9] This aspect of the line has baffled even H. R. Loyn: "In 'Beowulf' itself the good king is said to have distributed things to young and old, except the folk-share and the lives of men, that is to say, presumably, the land and people in general upon which the well-being of the kingdom depended." See H. R. Loyn, *Anglo-Saxon England and the Norman Conquest* (London: Longman, 1962), p. 207.

[10] See *Exodus* ll. 16-18 in *The Junius Manuscript*, ASPR I, ed. George Krapp (New York: Columbia University Press, 1931), p. 91. I am indebted to Charles Wright for suggesting the relevance of this passage.

[11] Susan Reynolds, "Bookland, Folkland and Fiefs," *Anglo-Norman Studies* 14 (1991), pp. 211-27.

yards and slaves, even when the disposition will have been made without a written document and in the presence of witnesses").[12]

The collocation of lands and men in *Beowulf* also occurs in Bede. The *Ecclesiastical History* is the first English source to describe a situation that becomes more or less familiar in later charters—the donation of laborers along with the lands they worked.[13] King Æthelwealh's donation of Selsey to archbishop Wilfrid includes unambiguously the people who live there: Æthelwealh donates "omnes qui ibidem erant, facultates *cum agris et hominibus*" ("all that was there, the resources along with the lands and the men").[14] Without mentioning *Beowulf*, N. J. Higham notes that the donation to Wilfrid narrated by Bede would appear to be our sole evidence from this era that transfers of estates included the people who occupied them.[15] As Stenton has observed, there is certainly no question that slaves "were normally regarded as part of the equipment of the lord's demesne."[16] It is thus not difficult to see why collocations of lands and men would occur in charters and legislation, nor is it difficult to imagine that such a colloca-

---

[12] See *Lex Visigothorum*, MGH Leges Sectio I, ed. Karl Zeumer (Hanover: Hahnsche Buchhandlung, 1935), p. 50. My italics.

[13] For grants of slaves along with land see *Anglo-Saxon Charters*, ed. and trans. A. J. Robertson (Cambridge: Cambridge University Press, 1939), LXXVII (p. 150), LXXIX (154), IV (Appendix, "Miscellaneous Documents," pp. 54-55).

[14] *Bede's Ecclesiastical History of the English People*, eds. Bertram Colgrave and R. A. B. Mynors (Oxford: Clarendon Press, 1969), pp. 374-75 (IV.13). The phrase corresponds to the formula *cum victu et cum hominibus* ("with the food and the men"), rendered in Old English as *mid mete and mid mannum*, found in a multitude of pre-conquest charters. See David A. E. Pelteret, *Slavery in Early Mediæval England* (Woodbridge: Boydell, 1995), p. 167. Pelteret observes that charters containing this formula often leave ambiguous the legal status of the persons transferred along with the land.

[15] See N. J. Higham, *An English Empire: Bede and the Early Anglo-Saxon Kings* (Manchester: Manchester University Press, 1997), p. 230.

[16] See F. M. Stenton, *Anglo-Saxon England*, 3rd ed. (Oxford: Oxford University Press, 1971), p. 469.

tion might have found its way into *Beowulf* in the discussion of Hrothgar's plans for Heorot. At the very least, assuming line 73 to constitute such a collocation would appear to make better sense of the evidence than most prior proposals, many of which advise emendation as a remedy to the difficulties posed by this passage.

### *Folcland* AND THE *Folcscaru*

What the discussion above makes clear is that *Beowulf* l. 73, far from being an isolated and eccentric passage, in fact has historical parallels that are still unacknowledged in the standard editions. For this reason the line is unlikely to be corrupt or interpolated. What remains is the question why, if royal donations of land and men were the norm throughout pre-conquest England, *Beowulf* tells us only that Hrothgar could not make such donations. At the center of this problem is the meaning of the deceptively transparent compound *folcscaru*, glossed as "public land" in Klaeber's edition. It is seldom realized that Klaeber's definition of *folcscaru* is quite novel in *Beowulf* scholarship. E. V. K. Dobbie notes that the interpretation of *folcscaru* as "public land" first enters *Beowulf* scholarship through Klaeber's edition, though it does not originate with him.[17] This gloss of *folcscaru* can only have been derived (though Klaeber does not mention the connection) from a few brief references to *Beowulf* in John Kemble's *Codex Diplomaticus Aevi Saxonici*, in which he takes the term to be a virtual synonym for *folcland*.[18]

---

[17] See Dobbie, ed., *Beowulf*, p. 119.

[18] *Codex Diplomaticus Ævi Saxonici*, 5 vols., ed. J. M. Kemble (London: Sumptibus Societatis, 1839-48), I, civ n. 24 and II, ix. The assumption that the occurrence of *folcscaru* in *Beowulf* has something to do with *folcland* remains standard to the present: see H. R. Loyn's entry for *folcland* in the *Reallexikon der Germanischen Altertumskunde*, eds. Johannes Hoops *et al.* (Berlin: De Gruyter, 1995), IX, 312. Kemble's own edition of *Beowulf* (2 vols., London: William Pickering, 1837) translates *folcscaru* as "the territory" (II, 4) and repeats Jakob Grimm's definition of *folcland* (see

Klaeber's new gloss for *folcscaru* departs markedly from the attempts of prior scholars. Though elsewhere in Old English verse and prose the term is taken to mean "nation," *folcscaru* as it occurs in *Beowulf* l. 73 clearly must mean something else.[19] Richard Heinzel first observed in 1889 that the gloss for *folcscaru* as "nation," familiar since William Somner's dictionary of 1659, requires in *Beowulf* the ungainly translation that Hrothgar gave everything "but the nation and the lives of men."[20] The seemingly analogous term *leodscaru* in the Old English *Exodus* (l. 337) is not especially helpful, as it is treated similarly in the standard dictionaries, usually defined as "nation."[21]

Klaeber's solution to the crux in *Beowulf* l. 73 can probably be improved upon. Since Kemble's discussion of *folcscaru* has gone virtually unexamined since the 1840s, scholars may want to hesitate before allowing it to survive without some sort of editorial proviso into contemporary editions of *Beowulf*.

below, n. 27) in his gloss of the term "sceran." Presumably his understanding of *Beowulf* l. 73 had evolved somewhat by the time he began work on the *Codex Diplomaticus*.

[19] The traditional definition of *folcscaru* has a long history, preserved from the entry for *folcsceare* in William Somner, *Dictionarium Saxonico-Latino-Anglicum* (London: Daniel White, 1659) to Grein-Köhler's *Sprachschatz der Angelsächsischen Dichter* (Heidelberg: Carl Winter, 1912), p. 205. While the latter defines *folcscaru* as "natio, provincia," the editors do briefly take note of Kemble's suggested definition.

[20] Richard Heinzel, "Moritz Heyne's *Beowulf*," p. 189. For a typical example of what might be called the "late" poetic usage of *folcscaru* see ll. 402 and 967 of Cynewulf's *Elene* (*The Vercelli Book*, ASPR II, ed. George Krapp [New York: Columbia University Press, 1932]). In both instances the term can only mean "nation." *Beowulf*'s apparent requirement that this noun mean something other than "nation" is unique in the Old English corpus.

[21] *The Junius Manuscript*, ed. Krapp, p. 100. See also the entry for *leodscearu* in James Bosworth and T. Northcote Toller, *An Anglo-Saxon Dictionary* (Oxford: Clarendon Press, 1898), p. 631.

Over the past century Kemble's views on the meaning of line 73 have raised suspicions among several Anglo-Saxonists.[22] In her 1948 address to the Royal Historical Society, Dorothy Whitelock questioned whether "the troublesome *Beowulf* line 'except the *folcscaru* and the lives of men'" can in fact tell us anything about the legal-historical problem of *folcland*.[23] It is unfortunate that Whitelock never followed with an investigation of her own.

Whitelock appears to have been repeating a suggestion made much earlier by Felix Liebermann that the equation of *folcscaru* with *folcland* in Kemble's *Codex Diplomaticus* might be implausible.[24] Whitelock's query has apparently been answered only by a long note in Eric John's *Land Tenure in Early England*, in which he concludes that the poem "gives no warrant for supposing that the *folcscearu* was land normally granted out to a king's companions."[25]

Ostensibly there is nothing objectionable about the putative similarity between the *folcscaru* and *folcland*, since both can apparently designate "nation" or "homeland" in Old English verse.[26] Kemble's discussion, however, refers unmistakably to

---

[22] On the role of Kemble in establishing German philological methods in England see Raymond A. Wiley, "Grimm's *Grammar* Gains Ground in England, 1832-52," in Antonsen, ed., *The Grimm Brothers and the Germanic Past*, pp. 33-42.

[23] Dorothy Whitelock, "Anglo-Saxon Poetry and the Historian," *Transactions of the Royal Historical Society* 31 (1949), pp. 75-94 at p. 93.

[24] See entry for *folcland* in Felix Liebermann, ed., *Gesetze*, II, 403.

[25] Eric John, *Land Tenure in Early England* (London: Leicester University Press, 1960), p. 53 n. 1. The discussion of *folcscaru* as it occurs in *Beowulf* is a minor point in John's study and is thus not supported with much evidence.

[26] The only occurrence of *folcland* in the Old English corpus, outside of its three occurrences in legal texts, is *Wife's Lament* l. 47. Here it can only mean "nation" or "homeland." The most recent edition appears in Fulk and Pope, eds., *Eight Old English Poems*.

the legal definition of *folcland*. That it does, as Stanley has observed, is a problem in itself.[27] By explaining the meaning of *folcscaru* in *Beowulf* l. 73 by means of *folcland*, Kemble was attempting to supplement our knowledge of one enigmatic term with evidence that was, in many ways, no less mysterious. Since the inception of Old English studies in the sixteenth century, few words have been the cause of more controversy than *folcland*. Kemble's work on the *Codex Diplomaticus* was preceded by something of a loose consensus on the meaning of the term, with definitions having been conjectured by such figures as William Blackstone and Jakob Grimm. All discussions were ultimately indebted to the translation of *folcland* as "terra sine scripto possessa" ("land not held in writing") in William Lambarde's *Archaionomia* (1568), a definition which was later expanded upon in Henry Spelman's posthumous *Glossarium Archaiologicum* (1664) as "terra popularis, communi iure et sine scripto possessa" ("land of the folk, held according to the common law and without a charter").[28]

Kemble's own discussion in the *Codex Diplomaticus* is notable for its surprising indifference to the interpretations of Blackstone, Grimm, Spelman and Lambarde, and the complications

[27] Without offering any solutions of his own, Stanley points out the difficulties of reconciling the current definition of *folcscaru* as it occurs in *Beowulf* l. 73 with the various definitions of *folcland* and *folcriht* in his "Courtliness and Courtesy in *Beowulf* and Elsewhere in English Medieval Literature," in *Words and Works: Studies in Medieval English Language and Literature in Honor of Fred C. Robinson,* eds. Peter S. Baker and Nicholas Howe (Toronto: Univ. of Toronto Press, 1998), p. 92.

[28] See the entry for *folcland* in Sir Henry Spelman and William Dugdale, *Glossarium Archaiologicum* (London: Alicia Warren, 1664), p. 236a; also William Lambarde, *Archaionomia* (London: 1568; reprint, Roger Daniel, 1644), f. 48. William Blackstone's interpretation of *folcland* is indebted to Spelman, but also adumbrates features of Allen's argument: See Blackstone, *Commentaries,* II, 91: "Folc-land . . . was held by no assurance in writing, but distributed among the common folk or people at the

that these would suggest for his exegesis of line 73. His approach to the explication of *folcland* is in fact decidedly controversial. Kemble drew his working definition of *folcland* not from the consensus view of his day but from what was then a recent polemic by John Allen, the *Inquiry into the Rise and Growth of the Royal Prerogative in England* (1830). Kemble and Allen seem to have shared certain ideological affinities that have not gone unnoticed in recent scholarship.[29] Both were anxious in much of their work to demonstrate the "democratic" and egalitarian character of Anglo-Saxon government; a view which, though by no means originating with them, was articulated in much of their work with a renewed forcefulness and a new presumption of scientific objectivity.

The myth of a primitive Germanic democracy flourishing before the incursions of Roman law was, of course, a convention of most legal-historical publications of the period; in its most essential aspects, it is traceable according to Kliger to the seventeenth century.[30] Benjamin Thorpe, also one of the first English antiquarians to adopt German and Danish philological methods, eulogized the Anglo-Saxon laws in the introduction to his *Ancient Laws and Institutes* in a manner similar to Kemble:

> Such then, as they appear in the following pages, were the Laws
> and Institutes of England, at the outset of her bright, though
> sometimes darkened course; what they would now have been,

pleasure of the lord." See also Jakob Grimm, *Deutsche Rechtsalterthümer*, p. 493: "*folcland* im gegensatz zu bocland . . . d.i. reine alod, im gegensatz zu beneficium, lehen." Kemble pointedly disagrees with the last definition: ". . . I differ from Grimm, who seems to consider *folcland* as the pure alod, *bocland* as the fief" (*Codex Diplomaticus*, I, civ-cv n. 24). The best overview of Spelman's work remains J. G. A. Pocock, *The Ancient Constitution and the Feudal Law*, chapter 5; for a brief discussion of the *folcland* controversy in the eighteenth and nineteenth centuries, see idem, pp. 384-85.

[29] See Patrick Wormald, *Making of English Law*, pp. 10-14.

[30] See Kliger, *Goths in England*, p. 80 and *passim*.

had Norman influence never had footing in the land, is a question difficult to answer, nor will the modern laws of the other Germanic nations supply us, by comparison, with the means of forming a plausible conjecture: the laws of imperial Rome having among them already in great measure supplanted their national institutes, at a period when those of the Anglo-Saxons still retained their Teutonic character, unimpaired by the calamities with which their empire had from time to time been assailed, and by which it was finally overthrown.[31]

What Kemble was able to bring to the old discussion of the freedoms enjoyed by the ancient Germanic peoples, steeped as he was in Jakob Grimm's studies, were new modes of demonstrating the ways in which the primitive communalism of Germanic government clashed with Roman notions of monarchical authority that would eventually gain ascendancy on the Continent. According to Kemble, land laws were of central importance in demonstrating the democratic character of primitive Germanic government, given their apparent dependence on notions of communal ownership.[32] Kemble's desire for evidence of primitive English communalism probably ac-

[31] Thorpe, *Ancient Laws and Institutes of England* (London: Eyre and Spottiswoode, 1840), p. x. A correspondent of Kemble's, Thorpe was one of the first editors to print Old English texts in Roman type, using special characters only for the dental fricatives, a development which represents scholars' growing mastery of Old English grammar as well as the influence of Jakob Grimm. What seems like a minor development to modern eyes in fact represented a rejection of the manner of editing Old English texts characteristic of the English "antiquarian" school that had dominated the study of early English prior to Kemble. See Wiley, "Grimm's *Grammar*," pp. 36-37.

[32] See Kemble, *Codex Diplomaticus*, I, iv: "The typical principle of Roman law was 'the property or land of the individual citizen, the *ager*, bounded and defined by civil and religious ceremonies.' The typical principle on the contrary of the Teutonic law was 'the land held in common, in German

counts in no small way for his being among the first of many early adherents to Allen's argument that *folcland* was land held in common.[33] Although Allen had been the first to offer such an argument, the dominance of texts like Grimm's *Deutsche Rechtsalterthümer* in Germanist historiography guaranteed his thesis nothing but enthusiastic support.[34] That Allen's theory

the *gau:*' out of this, in its development or its disturbance, arose the democratic and elective, or the aristocratic and the monarchal power in Europe. The Roman law considered the individual member of the state, the citizen: the Teutonic law based itself upon the family bond. Caesar and Tacitus, having their eyes fixed on this essential difference, concur in declaring that the Germans allowed of no individual possession, but held all their lands in common." Kemble's arguments reflect the then-popular belief, later relentlessly attacked by Maitland, in the "primitive collectivism" of preliterate Germanic societies: see Stephen D. White, "Maitland on Family and Kinship," in *The History of English Law: Centenary Essays on 'Pollock and Maitland,'* Proceedings of the British Academy 89, ed. John Hudson (Oxford: Oxford University Press, 1996), pp. 104-6. Kemble's discussion is an important component of the "village community" tradition of eighteenth-century historiography: the best discussion remains that of J. W. Burrow, "'The Village Community' and the Uses of History in Late Nineteenth-Century England," in *Historical Perspectives: Studies in English Thought and Society in honour of J. H. Plumb,* ed. Neil McKendrick (London: Europa, 1974), pp. 255-84.

[33] See John Allen, *Inquiry into the Growth of the Royal Prerogative* (London: Richard and John Edward Taylor, 1830, repr. 1849), p. 135: "Folcland, as the word imports, was the land of the folk or people. It was the property of the community. It might be occupied in common, or possessed in severalty; and, in the latter case, it was probably parcelled out to individuals in the folcgemot. But while it continued to be folcland, it could not be alienated in perpetuity; and therefore, on the expiration of the term for which it had been granted, it reverted to the community, and was again distributed by the same authority."

[34] Grimm had contended that *Gesammteigenthum* or "communal ownership" was one of the central features of archaic Germanic law. According to

enjoyed such widespread approval is surprising nonetheless, given that it seems to have hinged on a somewhat naive theory of Old English word-formation, encapsulated in his assertion that "[f]olkland, as the word imports, was the land of the folk or people."[35] Acceptance of Allen's assumption that nominal compounds beginning in *folc* necessarily indicate the ownership of "the people" allowed Kemble to revise the standard definition of *folcscaru*, and argue that this term as well designated "the *terra fiscalis*, or public land, grantable by the King and his council, as the representatives of the nation."[36] In support of his equation of *folcscaru* and *folcland*, Kemble reiterated Allen's etymological argument, supplementing it with other examples that might make it appear more plausible:

> [T]he etymology of the word leads irresistibly to the conclusion which I adopt: *scearu*, share or portion, is used over and over again to denote the estate or land of a particular person; and *folc-scearu* is the general or public share, as *folcriht* is the public law . . . *folctoga* the public leader,—compounds in which *folc* is equivalent to *þeod* in such words as *þeodcyning, þeodsceaða, þeodloga*.[37]

Allen's revision of the theory of *folcland*, which had engendered a revised interpretation of *folcscaru*, led ultimately to a new interpretation of *Beowulf* 1. 73. The line was now held by Kemble to be evidence of the democratic and egalitarian character of

Grimm's comparison of ownership in common and in severalty, the former (*ungetheiltes eigenthum*) was inevitably the more archaic and antiquated (*alterthümlicher und veraltender*) of the two. The lands spoken of in chapter 26 of Tacitus' Germania, *ab universis per vices occupati*, "sind kaum anders zu erklären als durch gemeinland" ("are hardly explicable unless understood as common lands"). See Grimm, *Deutsche Rechtsalterthümer*, p. 495 and n. 1.

[35] Allen, *Inquiry*, p. 135. See above, n. 33.

[36] Kemble, *Codex Diplomaticus*, II, ix.

[37] Kemble, *Codex Diplomaticus*, II, ix. Here and elsewhere I have altered Kemble's italics to conform to contemporary usage.

Hrothgar's government, and of early Germanic government in general:

> Over the *folcland,* at first the king alone had no control; it must
> have been apportioned by the nation in its solemn meeting; ear-
> lier, by the shire or other collection of free men. In *Beowulf,* the
> king determines to build a palace and distribute in it to his comi-
> tes, such gold, silver, arms, and other valuables as God had given
> him, save the *folcsceare* [*sic*] and the lives of men—*butan folcsceare
> and feorum gumena*—which he had no authority to dispose of.[38]

Klaeber's edition dominated twentieth-century studies of the
poem; likewise, his glosses of *folcscaru* as "public land" and *folcriht*
as the right to public land resurface in every scholarly edition
of the poem subsequent to his own.[39] Wrenn and Bolton's edition—the only post-Klaeber edition to give line 73 more than a
glance—does so only to assert that *folcscaru* "looks back to the
ancient Germanic right of the people of a village to own certain
land for grazing as an inalienable due in common—a right still
partly preserved in our 'commons'."[40] Wrenn's reading of this
line makes the world of *Beowulf* seem more egalitarian than even
Kemble had originally intended. Kemble does not in fact maintain that the land designated by terms such as *folcland* and *folcscaru* was held in common, but rather that it was part of a national

[38] Kemble, *Codex Diplomaticus,* I, civ n. 24.

[39] The gloss is ubiquitous in twentieth-century editions of the poem,
including the most recent and most authoritative: see entry for *folcscaru* in
the glossary of Fred Robinson and Bruce Mitchell, eds., *Beowulf: An Edition
with Relevant Shorter Texts* (Malden, MA: Blackwell, 1998).

[40] C. L. Wrenn and W. E. Bolton, eds., *Beowulf* (Exeter: University of Exeter
Press, 1953 repr. 1996), p. 102. Wrenn was here continuing the tradition
of assuming the right of common to have had analogues in pre-conquest
land law. For earlier examples, see Sir Francis Palgrave, *History of the Anglo-
Saxons* (London: William Tegg, 1869), pp. 212-13; Frederic Seebohm, *The
English Village Community,* 4th ed. (London: Longmans, 1915), p. xiii.

fund of land that might be parceled out by the king and his *witan* or body of counselors.[41] If the *folc* can be said to possess the land, they do so only in a representative sense.[42]

## FOLCLAND AFTER KEMBLE

There can be no doubt that the standard interpretation of *Beowulf*ian *folcscaru* and *folcriht* is based primarily on arguments offered over a century and a half ago by Kemble, arguments that, it must be said, are now somewhat difficult to take seriously. Perhaps one of the strangest consequences of Klaeber's gloss of *folcscaru* is that it compels us to repeat an interpretation of *folcland* more characteristic of the early nineteenth century than the twentieth. Though Allen and Kemble's interpretation of *folcland* as "common" or "public land" has crept into every contemporary scholarly edition of *Beowulf* via the suggested anal-

---

[41] Indeed, one should be careful to point out that in identifying the Anglo-Saxons with "democratic" institutions, Kemble had in mind a particular kind of egalitarianism that had no affinities with socialism. Clare Simmons observes that Kemble's *Saxons in England* (1848) was received well in part "because it provided an alternative history to the myth, used by the Chartists, that England had originally been democratic, with no property qualification for voting—and, of equal concern in 1848, had had a socialist approach to property-ownership." According to Simmons, Kemble's work "reclaimed the Anglo-Saxon world for established order, as opposed to revolution. Kemble's Anglo-Saxons, indeed, seem moderate Whigs in their severance of Divine Right from the monarchy in combination with their continued respect for government by the propertied classes." See Simmons, *Eyes Across the Channel: French Revolutions, Party History and British Writing, 1830-1882,* Interdisciplinary Nineteenth-Century Studies 1 (Amsterdam: Harwood, 2000), p. 122.

[42] Kemble's view is reiterated in Felix Liebermann, *The National Assembly in the Anglo-Saxon Period* (Halle: Max Niemeyer, 1913), p. 73: "The witan . . . had to guard the disposition of crown domains against reckless squandering,

ogy with the *folcscaru*, this interpretation of *folcland* has not been accepted by the preponderance of historians for over a century. The dominance of Allen's thesis began to wane in 1893, with the publication of a famous article by Paul Vinogradoff that restored to the satisfaction of most legal historians the interpretations offered by Lambarde and Spelman. In Vinogradoff's own words, *folcland* designated not "the public land" but "the holding of an individual which is governed by the ancient folkright and, therefore, subject to restrictions which tend to preserve it as a family estate."[43] Land held by "ancient folkright" differed from *bocland* in that the latter could be freely alienated and bequeathed to the owner's choice of recipient, while the former was subject to customary rules of inheritance that kept land in families.

Perhaps most immediately interesting is what Vinogradoff has to say about language. A major component of Vinogradoff's

which would deprive future governments of the possibility of rewarding out of public property warriors and officers . . . They controlled the giving away of crown land, not as a circle of personal associates and vassals of the king, but as a national representation." Kemble's interpretation of *Beowulf* l. 73, repeated without attribution in Klaeber's edition, has been widely disseminated in Anglo-Saxon studies and framed most subsequent discussion of the poem. It is largely reiterated in M. J. Swanton, *Crisis and Development in Germanic Society 700-800: Beowulf and the Burden of Kingship*, Göppinger Arbeiten zur Germanistik 333 (Göppingen: Kümmerle Verlag, 1982), p. 36: "Putting aside the disputed matter of *folc-land*, there is still required to be a clear distinction maintained between personal property belonging to the individual who is king, and that belonging to the office he holds. The public fisc, *þeodgestreon*, is invested not in the person of the king, but in his office. When Hrothgar generously bestows on young and old all that he has, in Heorot, it is *buton folcsceare ond feorum gumena* (73). And everywhere during this early period, the will of the people, either expressed indirectly through the nation-in-arms or through the witan, exercised a considerable influence on the actions and policy of their rulers."

[43] Paul Vinogradoff, "Folkland," *English Historical Review* 24 (1893), pp. 10-11.

assault on the "public land" theory of *folcland* was his derisive critique of the speculative etymology employed by Allen and reiterated by Kemble:

> Are we compelled to treat the "folk" of this compound word as though it were a genitive of possession? If folkland must be the land of which the folk is the owner, must not bookland be the land of which the book is the owner? We may look to other words which have folk by way of prefix. We find for instance fol-cfrig; this does not mean free man of the people, it means the man who is free by folkright, the man free under the ordinary law, the common law. With all due respect for those who have made a special study of the Anglo-Saxon language, I venture to suggest that folkland need not mean the land owned by the people. Bookland is land that his held by bookright: folkland is land that is held by folkright.[44]

Vinogradoff's discussion of *folcland* profoundly affected the study of Anglo-Saxon history over the last century.[45] The assumption that nominal compounds whose first element is *folc* necessarily indicate the ownership of the people (whoever "the people" might be) has rarely been taken seriously in subsequent legal-historical studies. The implications for *Beowulf* seem clear.

[44] Vinogradoff, "Folkland," p. 11.

[45] Few subsequent surveys of Anglo-Saxon land law fail to give at least grudging assent to his proposals, though attempts have been made to recuperate (only with major qualifications) the theories of Kemble and Allen. For modern restatements of Vinogradoff's thesis, see T. F. T. Plucknett, "Bookland and Folkland," *Economic History Review* 6 (1936), 64-72; F. M. Stenton, *Anglo-Saxon England*, pp. 307-12; H. R. Loyn, *Anglo-Saxon England and the Norman Conquest*, pp. 170-9. For the attempts to recover some aspects of Allen and Kemble's interpretation of *folcland* see Eric John, *Land Tenure in Early England*; idem, *Orbis Brittaniae and Other Studies* (London: Leicester University Press, 1966); Hanna Vollrath-Reichelt, *Königsgedanke und Königtum bei den Angelsachsen bis zur Mitte des 9. Jahrhunderts*, Kölner

There is no longer anything self-evident about the proposition that *folcscaru* designates "public land," as natural as this assumption may once have seemed to Allen and Kemble. Indeed, it is possible that "public land" survives into the most recent editions of *Beowulf* primarily because of institutional barriers between literary and legal-historical scholarship, which allowed a very dated assumption to haunt critical editions of *Beowulf* longer than it might have.

Vinogradoff's article suggests clear reasons why Hrothgar would be unable to donate land designated by the term *folcscaru*. Of the evidence adduced by Vinogradoff, perhaps the most valuable for the explication of line 73 is a famous charter of the West-Saxon king Æthelwulf dating to 846, in which the king donates 20 hides of land to himself. Whitelock notes that the charter is crucial to understanding the distinction between *folcland* and *bocland*, since it implies "that until the king had an estate of his own formally 'booked' to him, he could not leave it or give it to whom he pleased, nor free it from tribute and services for the sake of his beneficiary."[46] To Stenton, the fact that Æthelwulf could not make a gift of land without first turning it into *bocland* seemed "a curious illustration of the limited range of conceptions which governed Old English land law in the ninth century."[47] However curious it may be, the charter of Æthelwulf is not our only example of such restraints: King Edgar

Historische Abhandlungen 19 (Cologne and Vienna: Böhlau Verlag, 1971), pp. 214-19. None of the critiques of Vinogradoff's thesis appear to have disturbed the consensus on the meaning of *folcland* which it engendered: his thesis survives without qualification in Ann Williams, "Land Tenure," in *The Blackwell Encyclopædia of Anglo-Saxon England*, eds. Michael Lapidge *et al.* (Malden, MA: Blackwell, 2001), p. 277.

[46] The charter is no. 88 in Whitelock, *EHD*, I, 481-483, and no. 298 in P. H. Sawyer, *Anglo-Saxon Charters: An Annotated List and Bibliography* (London: Royal Historical Society, 1968). It is generally judged to be authentic.

[47] See F. M. Stenton, *Anglo-Saxon England*, pp. 304-5.

grants an estate to himself in a charter of 963 for precisely the same purpose.[48] The customary assumption that *folcscaru* was a synonym for *folcland* thus leads to conclusions about the meaning of *Beowulf* l. 73 very different from those of Klaeber and Kemble. If Hrothgar could not bestow lands designated as *folcscaru*, it is probably not because they were owned by "the public," but because they were, as the poet says, his own possessions.

Why would Hrothgar be prevented from giving away his own lands? The reasons become clear when we examine some of the continental analogues of *folcland*. Requirements that certain types of land remain within families figure prominently in Frankish legislation. While the means certainly existed within customary law for the selection of an heir outside one's kin, Frankish legislation stipulates that ancestral or patrimonial lands, called variously *terra salica* and *hereditas aviatica*, were to remain exclusively within the family, forbidden to pass even to close female kin while male relatives still lived.[49] Land that was not "ancestral" was transferred by an elaborate legal ritual, culminating in the throwing of a stick into the lap of the grantee known in Frankish legislation as *in laisum jactare.*[50] In a later article, Vinogradoff contends that the "symbolic investiture by sod" frequently mentioned in Anglo-Saxon charters is an Insular parallel to this ritual, and discusses extensively the customary practices surrounding land transfers which seem to have

[48] Edgar's charter is no. 715 in Sawyer, *Anglo-Saxon Charters*. It is also assumed to be authentic.

[49] *Lex Ribuaria* 57.4: "Sed dum virilis sexus exteterit, femina in hereditate aviatica non succedat" ("But while a man lives, a woman may not succeed to the ancestral landed inheritance"). See *Lex Ribuaria*, MGH Leges Sectio I, eds. Franz Beyerle and Rudolf Buchner (Hanover: Hansche Buchhandlung, 1954), p. 105. The translation is from *Laws of the Salian and Ripuarian Franks*, ed. and trans. Theodore John Rivers (New York: AMS Press, 1986), p. 192.

[50] For descriptions of the ritual see *Pactus Legis Salicae* 47, *Lex Ribuaria* 50, in Rivers, *Laws*, pp. 92-94 and 190, respectively.

survived into the literate era.[51] Vinogradoff asserts that these alienations could occur only with property that had already undergone "emancipation from the strict rules as to the claims of family and kindred excluding the power of disposal by individual owners."[52] Land governed by these traditional restraints thus could not be "given" at all. The charters of Æthelwulf and Edgar almost certainly reflect a mode of tenure characteristic of preliterate law, one that probably accounts for the restraints placed on Hrothgar in line 73.

Even the celebrated reference in Tacitus to lands *ab universis per vices occupati*, which for Grimm and others stood as irrefutable proof of Germanic communalism, may in fact be more ambivalent as evidence of such a situation than is routinely assumed. Richard Koebner observed in 1966 that buried in this passage is an attempt to throw cold water on earlier and somewhat less restrained speculations by Caesar on the egalitarian nature of Germanic land tenure. Koebner observes that, since the land under discussion has recently been captured, it can have been held "collectively" for only a brief period, after which it very clearly becomes individual property. Koebner's discussion is one of the few to consider Tacitus's observations critically, and merits quotation *in extenso*:

> The land settled by a tribe is what the tribe acquired collectively, what it acquired by conquest. For a time it might be held collectively, until the members of the tribe had come to an agreement about individual claims. The division once made was permanent: free trade in land was unknown. But Tacitus emphasized the fact that the act of division did really create individual property, which belonged to the holder and his heirs in perpetuity. And he does not fail to note that the shares are

---

[51] See Paul Vinogradoff, "Transfer of Land in Old English Law," *Harvard Law Review* 20 (1906-7), pp. 532-48 at p. 539.

[52] Vinogradoff, "Transfer of Land," p. 539.

not equal: *secundum dignationem,* according to his social rank, is the way in which an individual's claims are weighed. Here Tacitus is making another literary point; he is correcting the most famous of writers about the Germans without mentioning him. Caesar had maintained that a German had no property in land: the land was redivided yearly among family groups with a view to avoiding inequality (*G.B.* VI, c. 22). Well, Divus Julius was mistaken, Tacitus implies (. . .) In the definite sharing out of the land, as described by Tacitus, it is not a group of kindred, a clan, but the individual tribesman who appears as proprietor, *with the obligation to hand on his share to his descendants.*[53]

There is another apparent continental parallel to the provisions of *Beowulf* l. 73, this one pertaining not to land but to possessions acquired in war. A passage from Gregory of Tours suggests that Clovis himself was obliged to follow customary rules of ownership, this time governing the distribution of moveable property.[54] While still a pagan, Clovis ordered the sacking of a church, and his army took from it a ewer so precious to the bishop that he begged Clovis to return it. Clovis responded by asking the bishop to accompany him to Soissons, where the loot was to be divided up. Only if the ewer should be judged a part of Clovis's share, he asserted, could he return it to the bishop

[53] Richard Koebner, "The Settlement and Colonization of Europe," in *The Cambridge Economic History of Europe I: The Agrarian Life of the Middle Ages,* ed. M. M. Postan (Cambridge: Cambridge Univ. Press, 1966), p. 16. My italics.

[54] In 1892 Francis Gummere (*Germanic Origins,* pp. 289-90) extrapolated a Germanic custom from the following narrative of Clovis without comparing the passage to *Beowulf* l. 73: "Even of booty and plunder in war the king might take no more than his share as a warrior, and the division was not one of choice: it was all left to the lots. It is on the margin between the old dispensation and the new rule of kings that we meet that famous vase of Soissons."

("Cumque mihi vas illud sors dederit, quae papa poscit, adimpleam").[55] As the scene begins, Clovis beseeches his retainers with the following speech:

> "Rogo vos, o fortissimi proeliatores, ut saltim mihi vas istud" – hoc enim de urceo supra memorato dicebat – "extra partem concidere non abnuatis." Haec regi dicente, illi quorum erat mens sanior aiunt: "Omnia, gloriose rex, quae cernimus, tua sunt, sed et nos ipsi tuo sumus dominio subiugati. Nunc quod tibi bene placitum viditur facito; nullus enim potestati tuae resistere valet." Cum haec ita dixissent, unus levis, invidus ac facilis, cum voce magna elevatam bipennem urceo inpulit, dicens: "Nihil hinc accipies, nisi quae tibi sors vera largitur."[56]

> "I ask you, o most powerful warriors, that you might at least not refuse to grant me this vessel beyond my share." When the king had finished, they who were of cooler heads said, "Everything, magnificent king, that we have is yours, yea even we ourselves are subjugated to your authority. Now do what seems appropriate to you, for nothing can resist your power." When they said this, a certain inconstant, jealous and flippant man brought down upon the ewer a raised axe, saying with a great voice: "You will take nothing from here, unless it is granted to you as your true share."

One of the more remarkable things about Clovis's request that the ewer be ceded to him "beyond his share" (*extra partem*) is that it should be made at all. That it was (in so far as we can trust Gregory's account), and that it should be delivered in a pleading tone otherwise uncharacteristic of Clovis, indicates that Clovis was here compelled to maneuver within a system of norms that he had never chosen and which he could violate only at risk to

---

[55] See *Gregorii Episcopi Turonensis Libri Historiarum*, MGH Scriptorum Rerum Merovingicarum I, ed. Bruno Krusch (Hanover: Hahnsche Buchhandlung, 1950), p. 71 (II.27).

[56] Ibid.

himself and his authority. It is not hard to imagine that Hrothgar as well may have been viewed as a king obliged to observe similar restraints. It might also be said, though the point is admittedly conjectural, that this passage suggests a stage in the vocabulary of loot-distribution: words such as *pars* and *sors* may have rendered the Germanic vernacular cognates of OE *scaru* or *folcscaru*.

### POST-VINOGRADOFF DISCUSSIONS

There has been only one major counterproposal to Vinogradoff's argument over the last century, and while its conclusions are not widely accepted, it may nonetheless have something to tell us about *Beowulf* l. 73. Eric John's discussion of *folcland* was first published in 1966, and its major points are briefly reiterated in a more recent publication.[57] John suggests that the principal problem with Allen and Kemble's interpretation of *folcland* as "land of the people" is that it leaves unclear what is meant by "people."[58] He observes that when it is used as a poetic term, *folc* "is a frequent synonym for *fyrd* or even *here*," i.e., it is (much like *leod*, also a productive basis of poetic compounds) a poetic term for the warrior band.[59] To substantiate this point, John mentions only one example from Old English verse, *The Battle of Maldon*. Of the eight instances of *folc* in this text, "in five places it means army unambiguously, either the English or the Viking host."[60] From this evidence, John concludes that the land referred to by *folcland* is the land mentioned in Bede's letter to Egbert, the

---

[57] See John, *Reassessing Anglo-Saxon England* (Manchester: Manchester University Press, 1996), p. 49 n. 38.

[58] John, *Orbis Brittaniæ*, p. 118.

[59] John, *Orbis Brittaniæ*, p. 121.

[60] John, *Orbis Brittaniæ*, p. 121. The examples adduced by John from *The Battle of Maldon* are ll. 45, 202, and 54. See also D. H. Green, *Language and History in the Early Germanic World* (Cambridge: Cambridge University Press, 1998), pp. 90-91. Green concludes, particularly from Old High German evidence, that *folk* "pointed to a fighting formation smaller than the army."

71

land set aside by the state for military figures.[61] Thus, according to John, while Allen may have been more or less correct in seeing the *folcland* as a national fund of land, he was mistaken about its intended recipients, who were the warrior class and not the common people.

While it is worth avoiding any excessively precise definitions of Old English poetic terms, there is certainly reason to think that John's arguments about the usage of *folc* in heroic poetry are applicable to *Beowulf*. Admittedly, the evidence may not be as strong as one would like. Lines in which *folc* can only mean "army" may be more or less numerous than we will ever know, though they may be more scarce in *Beowulf* than in *The Battle of Maldon*: the only examples I am aware of (ll. 1422, 2948) are not decisive. But the frequent presence of a military meaning for *folc* in *Beowulf* would mean only that the poem's vocabulary was consistent with that of other Germanic heroic verse; indeed, the total absence of such a meaning would make *Beowulf* somewhat anomalous. The standard definitions of poetic compounds and phrases such as *folctogan* and *folces hyrde*—"leader" and "shepherd of the people," respectively—may have more to do with the political biases of early-twentieth century Germanic philology than with our empirical knowledge of early medieval economies and societies. A recent article by Josephine Bloomfield demonstrates that Klaeber's glosses consistently reflect an authoritarian ideology alien to the twenty-first century, and, more importantly, to the poem itself.[62]

Should *folc* sometimes mean "army" or "band of warriors" in more instances than previously assumed, then terms like *folcscaru* and *folcland* may have once been more strongly associated with military land before acquiring a more abstract meaning

---

[61] John, *Orbis Brittaniae*, p. 121.

[62] Josephine Bloomfield, "Benevolent Authoritarianism in Klaeber's *Beowulf*: An Editorial Translation of Kingship," *Modern Language Quarterly* 60 (1999), pp. 129-59.

characteristic of later charters and royal codes. John's arguments may well suggest something about the etymologies of compounds in *folc-* where they were used to denote possessions in land. Nonetheless, John's argument does not seem to warrant a substantial revision of the present consensus concerning the possible significance of *folcland* and seemingly analogous compounds. There are few reasons to doubt that family land received the same legal treatment whether or not it was owned by a family that had passed out of regular military obligations.

## CONCLUSIONS

While the simplicity of John's proposal is attractive, ultimately it is Vinogradoff's arguments that invite a wider discussion of the legal nature of *folc-*compounds in *Beowulf*. *Folcriht*, for example, is attested throughout Anglo-Saxon legislation, though never with the meaning ascribed by Klaeber, "legal share of the 'common' estate."[63] The standard definition remains that of Felix Liebermann, "Gemeinrecht im Gegensatz zum Königsrecht," i.e., the popular or common law, in contrast to written law and royal fiat.[64] The single attestation of the term in *Beowulf* (l. 2608) clearly requires that *folcriht* mean something else. But Klaeber's dependence on Kemble and nineteenth-century speculations about Germanic communalism obscures its potential connection with the written sources discussed in this essay. Here the usage of *folcriht* seems explicitly connected with the notion of ancestral land. Wiglaf recalls that Beowulf had granted him "wicstede weligne / Wægmundinga // folcrihta gehwylc, / swa his fæder ahte" ("the fine dwelling of the Wægmundings, each of the folk-rights which his father had possessed"). Keeping in mind the legal meaning of *folc*, it would seem that what Beowulf has done is not grant Wiglaf

[63] The translation of *folcriht* as "common law" has a long history: see E. G. Stanley, *Die angelsächsische Rechtspflege*, pp. 37-39.

[64] See entry for *folcriht* in Felix Liebermann, ed., *Gesetze*, II, 73.

a share of the "common land," but confirm him in his right to a portion of the ancestral land of the Wægmunding clan, of which both Beowulf and Wiglaf were members.[65]

Here it is difficult to tell whether Beowulf is acting as keeper of the patrimonial land or as king. Overseeing the dispensation of others' ancestral land certainly seems to have been one of the typical duties of an Anglo-Saxon king. Such is the import of a ninth-century charter drawn up for a lord Ælfred, who beseeches the king to allow his probably illegitimate son Æthelwald to inherit an unspecified portion of Ælfred's *folcland* in addition to three hides of *bocland*.[66] In either case, Beowulf's "gift" to Wiglaf obeys the requirements that I have argued govern Hrothgar's powers of alienation in line 73. Should he be acting as guardian of the ancestral lands, Beowulf has not given away the *folcland* but administered its distribution within his own kin-group. Thus the donation is not comparable to those described in Bede's letter to Egbert, in which grants of land were offered as inducements to wandering soldiers.

It could be objected that Hrothgar, if he lived at all, lived in an age of solely oral transactions; that, for this reason, to suggest that an implicit distinction between *boc* and *folc* like that described by Vinogradoff obtains in *Beowulf* can only mean that the poet engaged in anachronism. If he did, it is an anachronism also engaged in by the Alfredian translator of Bede's *Eccle-*

---

[65] The nature of Beowulf's relationship to the Wægmunding clan is unclear. Wiglaf is customarily assumed to be Beowulf's nephew. Norman Eliason contends that the poet has deliberately obscured the nature of the relationship for what he takes to be "artistic" purposes. See "Beowulf, Wiglaf and the Wægmundings," *ASE* 7 (1978), pp. 95-105. Klaeber seems to have been aware that the land received by Wiglaf is "hereditary land:" see his *Beowulf,* p. 272.

[66] "ꞇ gif se cyning him geunnan wille þæs folclandes to ðæm boclonde, þonne hæbbe he ꞇ bruce." See Sweet, ed., *A Second Anglo-Saxon Reader,* pp. 216-17. The interpretation of the passage given in this essay is identical to the one offered by Vinogradoff in "Folkland," pp. 9-11.

*siastical History* when he tells us that in 655 Oswy gave *bocland* to the Church in return for his victory against Penda.[67] Here *bocland* translates *possessionunculis terrarum,* a term that does not necessarily refer to land conveyed by a written charter.[68] That Oswy could have made a donation of chartered land seems impossible according to what is known about the history of charters in England. F. M. Stenton argued in 1954 that no lands were conveyed by charter in England before the achbishopric of Theodore of Tarsus, who was consecrated in 668 and afterwards adapted Roman charters to unwritten English practice.[69] Charters of kings who ruled before this time, such as those attributed to Æthelberht, have been shown without exception to be fabrications.[70]

Viewing the attestation of *folcscaru* in *Beowulf* l. 73 as a reference to "ancestral lands" has clear advantages over the standard interpretation. The belief in primitive Germanic communalism so characteristic of nineteenth-century historiography now

[67] See *The Old English Version of Bede's Ecclesiastical History of the English People,* EETS o.s. no. 96, ed. and trans. Thomas Miller (London: Oxford University Press, 1890-98 repr. 1959-63), pp. 234-36: "Ond he þa gehet, gif Drihten him sige sellan wolde, þæt he wolde his dohtor Gode forgeofan & gehalgian in clænum mægðhade; ond swelce eac twelf boclanda æhte þæt he Gode geaf mynster on to timbrenne: & swa medmicle weorode þæt he to þam campe ferde." The phrase *possessionunculis terrarum* is glossed as *bocland* in an early Bede manuscript, Cotton MS. Tiberius C. ii., on fol. 83r. The glosses in this manuscript are printed in *Old English Glosses,* Modern Language Association of American General Series XVI, ed. Herbert Dean Meritt (New York: MLA, 1945), pp. 6-14.

[68] Or, in some manuscripts, simply *possessiones.* Bosworth notes that *bocland* translates the much less ambiguous *testamentum* in Alfred's *Orosius.* See the entry for *bocland* in Bosworth and Toller, *An Anglo-Saxon Dictionary,* p. 142.

[69] See F. M. Stenton, *The Latin Charters of the Anglo-Saxon Period* (Oxford: Clarendon Press, 1955), p. 31.

[70] See Richardson and Sayles, *Law and Legislation from Æthelberht to Magna Carta,* p. 160.

seems, as far as *Beowulf* and the interpretation of compounds in *folc-* is concerned, either an oversimplification of the complex nature of land tenure in early England or a naive imposition of modern institutions upon the poem. Future editors of *Beowulf* would do well to preserve its traces only when something better has not been made available. The somewhat less fantastic view that *folcscaru* refers to a national fund of land, often insufficiently distinguished from the communalist interpretation mentioned earlier, is likewise unsatisfying, since it does not explain why an otherwise legitimate power of Germanic kings is restricted in line 73. This reading also requires that we disregard the poet's own assertion that the *folcscaru* belonged not to the nation but to Hrothgar himself; land that was to be distributed to soldiers would seem not to have been governed by the sort of prohibitions implied by line 73. The belief that the *folcscaru* was a national fund of land is inevitably an inference motivated not by the text of the poem but by later notions of kingship and the state whose presence in *Beowulf* cannot be proven. The interpretation advocated in this chapter links *Beowulf* l. 73, an otherwise insoluble crux, with a substantial body of historical evidence, and a historiographical tradition much closer to contemporary sensibilities than that of Allen and Kemble.

We have seen how the ownership of land in common, or at least the absence of well-defined notions of personal property (often insufficiently distinguished from common pasture, some evidence of which does indeed exist in Old English sources) emerged in nineteenth-century commentary on *Beowulf* as one of the criteria of sociocultural primitivism.[71] The established scholarly habit of finding in Old English texts the seeds of modern freedoms (even vanishing ones), combined with the view that *Beowulf* preserves traces of archaic legal formulas, made possible the transformation of a relatively opaque compound in *folc-* into a testament to the ancient freedoms of the English

---

[71] Richard Koebner, "The Settlement and Colonization of Europe," pp. 37-42.

people. In the following chapters, we will see how other institutions came to be deployed as the criteria of primitivism, a development that likewise resulted from emerging knowledge of the "primitive" peoples who were becoming the objects of anthropological study. The master-narratives to which most legal historians subscribed regarding the fixed paths that sociocultural evolution might follow determined the attitudes that would prevail among students of *Beowulf* in the decades after Kemble's work. The status of *Beowulf* as a text disclosing the origins of English or Germanic institutions left post-Kemble philologists and legal historians with little doubt that the social world it describes was little different from present-day "primitive" societies as they were constructed within nineteenth-century ethnography. Both modern "primitives" and the populations depicted in *Beowulf* were held to inhabit a world governed by animistic views of nature and an irrational, consuming fascination with vengeance.

# III

## The Ecstasy of Vengeance:
## Nineteenth-century Germanism and the Finn Episode

FEW PORTIONS OF *Beowulf* have elicited a greater quantity of critical comment than the digression known as the "Finn Episode," a brief narrative of the battle between Hengest and Finn that is recited upon Beowulf's defeat of Grendel. The episode contains some of the most troublesome cruces of the poem and a number of passages that are hopelessly obscure without recourse to emendation.[1] Given its singular difficulties, it is surprising that this digression is routinely used in scholarship as evidence by which to assess attitudes toward the feud in Anglo-Saxon England. Particularly in the last century, considerable attention has been given to the question of whether the episode offers a positive or condemnatory view of vengeance. That the feud depicted in the episode is a kind of tragedy became a standard critical assumption in the early twentieth century with the publication of Henry Morgan Ayres's essay of 1917.[2] Speculations on the episode's tragic nature culminated in Martin Camargo's 1981 essay, which argued that the Finn Episode functions "to cast doubt on the revenge ethic at the very point in the narrative where such a code appears most glorious."[3] Camargo's

---

[1] The textual difficulties of the episode are reviewed in Donald K. Fry, ed., *Finnsburh Fragment and Episode* (London: Methuen, 1974), pp. 1-29. See also Andy Orchard, *A Critical Companion to* Beowulf (Cambridge: D. S. Brewer, 2003), pp. 173-87.

[2] Henry Morgan Ayres, "The Tragedy of Hengest in *Beowulf*," *JEGP* 16 (1917), pp. 282-95.

[3] Martin Camargo, "The Finn Episode and the Tragedy of Revenge in *Beowulf*," *Studies in Philology* 78 (1981), pp. 120-134 at p. 132.

views resurface in Greenfield and Calder's *New Critical History of Old English Literature* (1986), in which the episode is seen as revealing "the failure of human efforts to achieve peaceful compromise."[4] In his important 1995 study, John M. Hill takes issue with all such claims, contending that the poet's supposed disapproval of the feud is really an effect of our modern discomfort with vengeance and inability to appreciate its efficacy as a means of preserving social order:

> We think of revenge as something extralegal, as something to be replaced by systems of payment or some other form of non-lethal settlement, such as outlawing the offending person or party. But many societies, including Germanic societies, do not see revenge in exactly these ways; nor does the *Beowulf* poet in the world he dramatizes for us.[5]

All of these studies seem unconcerned that the feud is by no means a self-evident feature of the episode, as arguments for its presence frequently depend on tendentious readings of scant and often indeterminate evidence. For example, Wrenn and Bolton's note on ll. 1142-45 translates the compound *worold-ræden*—a somewhat mysterious *hapax legomenon*—as "the universally acknowledged duty (of vengeance)."[6] Klaeber had changed *worold-ræden* to *weorod-rædend*, "ruler of the host, king," an emendation that most contemporary scholarship has summarily rejected, presumably as a case of *Konjekturfreudigkeit*.[7] It should be said in Klaeber's defense that there is more evidence for the emendation of *ræden* to *rædend* than is mentioned in his note. Johannes Hoops's *Kommentar* compares *woroldrædenne* to MS *sele rædenne* (l. 51), which J. M. Kemble first suggested was

---

[4] Stanley Greenfield and Daniel Calder, *A New Critical History of Old English Literature* (New York: New York Univ. Press, 1986), p. 144.

[5] Hill, *Cultural World*, p. 29.

[6] Wrenn and Bolton, eds., *Beowulf*, p. 144 n. 1142-45.

[7] Klaeber, ed., *Beowulf*, pp. 175-76 n. 1142-45.

an error for *selerædende*.[8] Kemble's emendation is now standard, and is accepted even by Wrenn and Bolton, though not by the conservative Heyne-Schücking edition.

The restoration of *worold-ræden* and other words emended by Klaeber is crucial to William Ian Miller's important discussion, which presupposes that the situation described within the Finn Episode is unambiguously governed by the rules of the feud.[9] The *icge gold* mentioned after the description of the peace treaty is taken to be wergild, and Hengest's acceptance of the payment puts him at risk of becoming one of the ignominious *níðingar* of Germanic history who forswore vengeance and carried their deceased kinsmen "in their purses."[10] Miller does not mention Klaeber's assertion (repeated with approval by Hoops) that here "the payment of wergild seems out of the question," though his disagreement with Klaeber on this point does place him in the company of Dorothy Whitelock.[11] The poem's language is certainly more taciturn than either Miller or Whitelock indicates. The passage itself—"Að wæs geæfned, / ond icge gold // ahæfen

[8] Hoops, *Kommentar*, p. 144 n. 1142.

[9] William Ian Miller, "Choosing the Avenger: Some Aspects of the Bloodfeud in Medieval Iceland and England," *Law and History Review* 1 (1983), pp. 159-204.

[10] Miller, "Choosing the Avenger," p. 193. The allusion is to the common Icelandic phrase chiding those who accept a monetary settlement in exchange for vengeance: see e.g. *Austfirðinga sögur,* Íslenzk fornrit 11, ed. Jón Jóhanneson (Reykjavík: Hið íslenzka fornritafélag, 1950), p. 17: "Þorsteinn hvíti kvazk eigi vilja bera Þorgil, son sinn, í sjóði" ("Þorsteinn the White said that he would not bear Þorgil, his son, in (his) purse").

[11] Dorothy Whitelock, *The Audience of Beowulf* (Oxford: Clarendon, 1958 repr. 1970), p. 18: "I do not understand why Klaeber should pronounce so categorically that in the Finn episode the gold brought from the hoard after the oath was performed could not have been for the payment of wergild. It is difficult to see how Hengest and his party could have come to terms with Finn without a settlement being paid for Hnæf." For Klaeber's discussion of the passage see his *Beowulf,* p. 173 n. 1107-8.

of horde" ("The pyre [or oath] was made ready, and *icge* gold brought from the hoard")—leaves unclear precisely who receives the payment.[12] Should l. 1107a indeed be describing an "oath" (a reading that likewise puts one at odds with Grein, Klaeber and Hoops, as well as textual conservatives like W. W. Lawrence), it is an oath that is taken by both parties, and there is no obvious reason to assume that the payment might not be mutual as well.[13] Miller's definition of *worold-ræden* is less specific than that of Wrenn and Bolton, based largely on Arthur Brodeur's proposed glosses, "universal law" and "universal obligation."[14] Hunlafing's placement of a sword in the lap of Hengest is taken by Miller to be an attestation of the "egging" ritual of the Icelandic sagas, a custom that was "universal" among the Germanic peoples and perhaps the referent of *worold-ræden*.[15]

That Hunlafing's gesture constitutes a kind of symbolic action has, as Miller notes, been recognized by criticism for some time. Miller does not mention R. W. Chambers's discussion of the passage, however, which interprets the ceremonial gift of

---

[12] Klaeber, *Beowulf*, l. 1107. Klaeber describes *icge* as "entirely obscure" and so the term is left untranslated. Presumably arguments that the passage describes wergild payment are based on its putative resemblance to the language with which Hrothgar's feud settlement is described in ll. 470-72: "Siððan þa fæhðe / feo þingode; //sende ic Wylfingum/ofer wæteres hrycg//ealde madmas; /he me aþas swor" ("Then [I] settled the feud with money; I sent to the Wylfingas over the water's back old treasures; he swore oaths to me.")

[13] See W. W. Lawrence, "Beowulf and the Tragedy of Finnsburg," *PMLA* 30 (1915), pp. 372-431 at p. 406 n. 22, where he suggests the emendation of *að* "oath" to *ad* 'pyre,' and reads the payment as an exchange of treasure "appropriate to the sealing of a compact of peace."

[14] Miller, "Choosing the Avenger," p. 197 n. 151; Arthur Brodeur, "The Climax of the Finn Episode," *University of California Publications in English* 3 (1943), pp. 312-30 at pp. 329-30.

[15] "Yet it is possible that *woroldrædenne* refers more precisely to vengeance taken in response to the ceremony Hunlafing performs, the ceremony itself being a universal custom." Miller, "Choosing the Avenger," p. 197 n. 151.

the sword somewhat differently:

> The placing of the sword, by a prince, in the bosom of another,
> is a symbol of war-service. It means that Hengest has accept-
> ed obligations to a Danish lord, a Scylding, a kinsman of the
> dead Hnæf, and consequently that he means to break the troth
> which he has sworn to Finn.[16]

A persistent implication of many works mentioned above is
that interpretive problems posed by the Finn Episode are solu-
ble only within the system of obligations and rituals that make
up the feud. Though his emendations make application of feud
principles more difficult than scholars would like, Klaeber also
seems to assent passively to this view of the poem insofar as he
abstracts from the behavior of Hengest an essentially Germanic
duty of vengeance. According to Klaeber, the settlement agreed
to by Finn and Hengest was never acceptable, since "[m]aking
peace with the slayers of one's lord was entirely contrary to the
Germanic code of honor."[17] In support of this thesis, Klaeber
adduces a brief passage from the Cynewulf and Cyneheard
episode of the *Anglo-Saxon Chronicle,* while failing to mention
Ayres's caveat against such a comparison.[18]

[16] R. W. Chambers, *Beowulf: An Introduction to the Study of the Poem with
a Discussion of the Stories of Offa and Finn,* 3rd ed. with supplement
(Cambridge: Cambridge Univ. Press, 1967), p. 253.

[17] Klaeber, *Beowulf,* p. 173 n. 1102.

[18] "The alderman's godson, not to mention the British hostage, survived
the feud between Cynewulf and Cyneheard. This, the classical example
of loyalty to the ideal, is not altogether on all fours with the feud between
the Danes and the Frisians. For the followers of the dead Cynewulf to
take service with Cyneheard was to bestow on him the kingdom of which
they were the constituted authorities, if you please, and they may have
had all sorts of motives, besides the disinclination to follow their lord's
murderer which they chance to avow, by putting down civil war." Ayres,
"The Tragedy of Hengest in *Beowulf,*" p. 288.

The potential problems of the approach outlined above have not gone unnoticed in recent scholarship. Observing that the feud is conventionally understood as a means of preserving the peace, an "intra-social mechanism that is subject to settlement," David Day notes that "[m]ost English speakers considering the meaning of 'feud' would probably think of combat between armed bands of hillbillies living within a relatively small and isolated geographic area, not a clash of arms between sovereign political entities."[19] Criticism of the Finn Episode has sporadically recognized that the combat between Finn and Hengest's men may best be considered an example of the latter. Klaeber notes that the poem's point of view is "distinctly—almost patriotically—Danish," a remark which suggests that it is Danish fortunes in battle, and not the principle of vengeance in itself, with which the episode is primarily concerned.[20] Greenfield and Calder likewise observe that the episode's culmination in "a Danish victory" sufficiently explains its inclusion in *Beowulf*.[21]

The degree of violence in the Finn Episode also seems to argue against its routine classification as an instance of feuding. Day contends the *Beowulf* poet's notions of feuding are "notably *not* commensurate with modern models of feuding behavior," in that "few rules concerning the timing or scale of vengeance seem to be observed."[22] Miller has himself famously emphasized

---

[19] David Day, "*Hwanan Sio Fæhð Aras:* Defining the Feud in *Beowulf*," *PQ* 78 (1999), pp. 77-95.

[20] Fr. Klaeber, "Observations on the Finn Episode," *JEGP* 15 (1914), pp. 544-49 at p. 545. See also Alexander Green, "The Opening of the Episode of Finn in *Beowulf*," *Publications of the Modern Language Association* 31 (1916), pp. 759-97 at p. 760: "The circumstances attending the recital of the feud are noteworthy. The song is sung in a Danish court, before a Danish assemblage; and, altho[ugh] the real hero of the entire epic, Beowulf, is a Geat, the episode as well as the poem *Beowulf* is thr[o]u[gh]out a glorification of Danish prowess and adventure."

[21] Greenfield and Calder, *New Critical History*, p. 143.

[22] Day, "Defining the Feud," p. 79.

that the feud in Iceland and elsewhere usually was governed by
"a rough rule of equivalence in riposte" that permitted violence
only against certain persons, not all-out butchery of one's opponents.[23] With this in mind, Wrenn and Bolton's grasp of what
constitutes a feud (and that of most *Beowulf* scholarship itself)
is clearly somewhat more expansive. According to Wrenn and
Bolton's edition, when Hengest and his men "exterminate their
enemies" (i.e., Finn and his retainers), they have taken the "full
and final vengeance" with which the "feud is completed."[24]

Day's solution to the definitional problem of *fæhð* in *Beowulf*
is his contention that feuding "is not clearly distinguished in the
poem from other forms of violence, such as warfare and raid-
ing."[25] He goes on to conclude that the poet's use of the term

[23] Miller, *Bloodtaking and Peacemaking: Feud, Law and Society in Saga Iceland*
(Chicago: Univ. of Chicago Press, 1990), p. 181.

[24] Wrenn and Bolton, *Beowulf,* p. 145 n. 1146-51. The assumption that
Hengest kills Finn and his men in a state of feud can also cast a negative
light on the actions of the Danes should the incident be read in the context
of continental legislation. Chapter 27 of the *Lex Saxonum* (ed. C. F. von
Schwerin, MGH Leges 4 [Hanover: Hahnsche Buchhandlung, 1918, p. 25])
indicates that in killing Finn in his own hall, Hengest and his men violated
the king's "house peace." The rule remains valid even if the violence takes
place within the context of the feud: "Qui hominem propter faidam in
propria domo occiderit, capite puniatur" ("Let he who kills a man in his
own home because of a feud receive the highest punishment").

[25] Day, "Defining the Feud," p. 79. Day's solution was anticipated by
some remarks of Francis Gummere (*Germanic Origins*, pp. 179-180):
"Feud, which this system (i.e., wergild) was meant to lay aside, seems
to have been a wide word. It included the strained relations between
King Hrethel and his son, the murder of Abel, Grendel's direful raids
upon the hall "Heorot," and of course the hostility between two families
or clans, the private shedding of blood for blood." More recently, Paul
Hyams has noted that *Beowulf* "retained feud language even for what
we should certainly call wars;" see Hyams, "Feud in Medieval England,"
*Haskins Society Journal* 3 (1991), pp. 1-21 at p. 7.

*fæhð* indicates a definition of feud peculiar to the poem, encompassing forms of violence less stylized than the feuds analyzed by Miller though governed by an analogous system of rules. Interestingly enough, the fight between the Danes and Frisians in the Finn Episode is one of the few battles to which the poet does *not* apply the term *fæhð*. It is perhaps for this reason that Frederic Seebohm chose not to include the Finn Episode in his classic 1911 survey of the *Beowulf* poet's treatment of feud customs.[26] Nonetheless, Day's essay highlights an important problem of *Beowulf* studies, one whose relevance to the question of whether the Finn Episode can usefully be described as a feud is considerable. In *Beowulf* we often encounter terms and phrases that are demonstrably part of a technical legal vocabulary. But to what extent do they fulfill their technical function in *Beowulf?* Klaeber lists a number of legal terms that are employed merely figuratively in *Beowulf,* a view largely endorsed by E. G. Stanley.[27] The usage of the term *morð* and its Anglian variant *morðor* in *Beowulf* may prove more instructive, as compounds derived from the latter occur twice in the Finn Episode.[28] In legal usage, *morð* refers generally to the concealment of homicide. The distinction is more or less apparent in most examples of Germanic law, but it is especially clear in Scandinavian legal compilations, which maintain a meticulous distinction between secret, "criminal" homicide (*morð*) and homicide that is not followed by concealment (*bani, víg* or *dráp*).[29] According to Klaus von See, while

---

[26] Frederic Seebohm, *Tribal Custom,* pp. 56-72.

[27] Klaeber, ed., *Beowulf,* p. 272; E. G. Stanley, "Two Old English Poetic Phrases Insufficiently Understood for Literary Criticism: *þing gehegan and seonoþ gehegan,*" in Daniel Calder, ed., *Old English Poetry: Essays on Style* (Berkeley: Univ. of California Press, 1979), pp. 67-90.

[28] See Angus Cameron *et al.,* "A Reconsideration of the Language of *Beowulf,*" in Chase, ed., *The Dating of Beowulf,* p. 74.

[29] The most often-cited passages occur in chapters 87 and 88 of the thirteenth-century Icelandic compilation known as Grágás; see the edition of Vilhjálmur Finsen, *Grágás: Islændernes Lovbog i Fristatens Tid*

this technical distinction is maintained consistently in legislation and saga literature, in skaldic verse "*morð* often appears as
a term of praise for bloody warfare and *myrðir,* 'murderer,' as an
honorific epithet for the warrior and warlike prince."[30]

There have been attempts to see the usage of *morðor* in the
Finn Episode as consistent with its legal meaning, both of which
depend on the presence of feud.[31] But one might just as easily argue that *morðorbealo maga* (l. 1079) and *morðorhete* (l. 1105) both
show an heretofore unnoticed affinity with what von See argues
is the typical definition of the term in skaldic verse: "bloody war-

(Copenhagen: Berlings bogtrykkeri, 1852), pp. 153-54. The best-known
attempt to define *morð* occurs in chapter 88 (p. 154): "En þa er morð ef
maðr leynir eða hylr hræ eða gengr eigi í gegn" ("And that is murder if a
man conceals or hides the body, or does not confess").

[30] Klaus von See, *Altnordische Rechtswörter,* Hermæa 16 (Tübingen:
Max Niemeyer, 1964), p. 21: ". . . erscheint *morð* häufig als ehrende
Bezeichnung für den blutigen Kampf und *myrðir* 'Mörder' als ehrendes
Epitheton für den Krieger und kriegerischen Fürsten."

[31] Bruce O'Brien (*God's Peace and King's Peace: The Laws of Edward the
Confessor* [Philadelphia: Univ. of Pennsylvania Press, 1999], p. 79) has
recently argued that the term is used in *Beowulf* to describe "those
killings that could not be settled by compensation, but must inevitably
lead to a feud. In *Beowulf,* the bloody battle between Finn and Hnæf's
men, because it involved deception, led to many *morðras,* which doomed
the winter truce between the survivors to a spring of new slayings; these
*morðras* could only be answered 'by the edge of a sword'." Hill (*Cultural
World of* Beowulf, p. 26) likewise asserts that the term "'[m]urder-bale'
links what Hildeburh sees to what Grendel does, with what Hrothgar
accordingly feels, and with terrible kin-slaying. Thus Hildeburh's grief
and her bitterness about dark crime must cry for settlement." I am aware
of one attestation of the term that seems unambiguously tied to its legal
meaning, that of line 136a: for an extended discussion of this passage
see Stefan Jurasinski, "*Reddatur Parentibus:* The Vengeance of the Family
in Cnut's Homicide Legislation," *Law and History Review* 20 (2002), pp.
157-80 at pp. 178-79.

fare." Any explicit relation that either of these terms might have to the feud can be construed only with some difficulty.[32]

Chambers's discussion of the Finn Episode highlights just the sort of terminological problems outlined above when he argues against the customary interpretation of line 1102, "ðeah hie hira beaggyfan / banan folgedon" ("although they followed the slayer of their ring-giver"). Traditionally scholarship had assumed that the poet's use of *bana* referred strictly to Finn, and this feature of the episode was some of the primary evidence used to demonstrate Finn's responsibility for the feud. Chambers asserts that the conventional interpretation of *bana* demonstrates the routine use of excessively precise and loaded definitions of the term:

> I do not see how the fact that Finn is called the *bana* of Hnæf can prove anything as to "the blame for the attack." Of course the older editors may have thought so. Kemble translates *bana* "slaughterer," which implies brutality, and perhaps culpability. Bosworth-Toller renders *bana* "murderer," which certainly implies blame for attack. But we know that these are mere mistranslations. Nothing as to "blame for the attack" is implied by the term *bana:* "*bana* 'slayer' is a perfectly neutral word, and must not be translated by 'murderer,' or any word connoting criminality. A man who slays another in self-defence, or in righteous execution of the law, is still his 'bane.'" Everyone admits this to be true: and yet at the same time *bana* is quoted to prove that Finn is to blame; because, for want of a better word, we half-consciously render *bana* "murderer": and "murderer" does imply blame. "Words," says Bacon, "as a Tartar's bow, do shoot back upon the understanding of the wisest."[33]

---

[32] Benjamin Thorpe translates *morðorhete* as "deadly feud;" see his *Anglo-Saxon Poems of Beowulf, the Scop or Gleeman's Tale, and the Fight at Finnesburg* (Oxford: Clarendon, 1855 repr. 1875), l. 2214.

[33] Chambers, *Beowulf: An Introduction*, p. 271; quoted passage is from John Earle and Charles Plummer, eds., *Two of the Saxon Chronicles Parallel*, 2 vols. (Oxford: Clarendon), II, 47.

Chambers's discussion is an early complaint against the tendency of *Beowulf* scholarship to force the events of the Finn Episode into the context of the feud, a context that is overtly required, as the discussion above makes clear, by few if any features of the episode. Discomfort with scholars' dependence on such constructs as the feud and the Germanic code of honor has been articulated more recently by Richard North, who has argued more forcefully than any scholar for the inapplicability of the feud to the interpretation of the Finn Episode:

> If the "heroic code" had any place in this Episode, why did Hengest and the Danes strike a deal with the man responsible for Hnæf's death? Should they not have died around his body, instead? And yet no commentator, so far, has failed to use this unwritten code as a constant in determining the motives of these warriors in the Episode. In fact there is no evidence in this text that Hengest has any duty to avenge a leader who was not a blood-relative.[34]

Neither scholar inquires into why earlier scholarship should have insisted so pointedly on Finn's responsibility for the attack and for his status as a murderer, a move which transforms the ensuing battle from a simple insurrection of the Danes against the Frisians (the view that Chambers seems to endorse) to the pursuit of a bloodfeud—a form of revenge that is distinct in many ways from the sort of vengeance that would naturally be desired by a group of captive and humiliated warriors. In this chapter, I would like to suggest that there may be more at work here than the "half-conscious" rendering of slippery words. The reasons why *Beowulf* scholarship has been so unwilling to see the Finn Episode outside of the domain of feuding over the past century become clear when we examine the episode's critical heritage in light of nineteenth-century attitudes toward the

---

[34] See North, "Tribal Loyalties in the *Finnsburh Fragment* and Episode," *Leeds Studies in English* n.s. 21 (1990), pp. 13-43 at p. 25.

feud. Accordingly, I shall explore how many nineteenth-century scholars conceived of the feud and its implications for the study of literary texts. It should become clear that the tendency of contemporary scholarship to view the feud as the major tool of exegesis for the Finn Episode is demonstrably a reflex of nineteenth-century assumptions about the nature of early Germanic society, some of which are no longer tenable.

## NINETEENTH-CENTURY VIEWS OF THE BLOODFEUD

By the late nineteenth century, cultivation of feud customs had come to be seen as a basic and essential trait of Germanic culture. In itself, this is by no means an unsound point of view, and the evidence to be presented subsequently should not be construed as implying that the monuments of Germanic literary and legal culture do not show an extraordinary degree of interest in vengeance, or recognize it sporadically as a praiseworthy (but not legally acceptable) mode of dispute settlement. What is of interest in the following discussion is less the question of the extent to which early Germanic peoples were motivated by a desire for vengeance than the rhetoric—often somewhat unrestrained—surrounding nineteenth-century discussions of Germanic feud customs; rhetoric which often, it must be said, significantly exaggerated the importance of vengeance to Germanic lawmaking and literature. A historical survey that Klaeber thought "excellent," Francis Gummere's *Germanic Origins* (1892), contends that the feud is an outcome of the "ferocity of the Germanic temperament."[35] Everywhere in literary and historical records, Gummere finds evidence for the same "deep-rooted Germanic love of the feud, of bloodshed and revenge."[36] In another study, Gummere claims that even the meter of Germanic verse "inclines, like our ancestors themselves, to violence," its alliterative line "at its best in describing the din of

---

[35] Gummere, *Germanic Origins*, p. 181. See also Klaeber, *Beowulf,* clxxvi.

[36] Gummere, *Germanic Origins*, p. 181.

war" and "cadenced by the crashing blows of sword and axe."[37] The widespread assumption that love of the feud was somehow fundamentally Germanic probably influences Klaeber when he says that because of its emphasis on (among other themes) the "sacred duty of revenge," no Anglo-Saxon poem "equals the 'Finn tale' in its thorough Germanic and heroic character."[38]

Sentiments such as these are so typical of historical and philological scholarship in the late nineteenth century (and, to some extent, in the twentieth) that it is difficult to imagine *Beowulf* scholarship without them. It is thus surprising to observe the lack of interest in the feud in such a foundational text of early Germanist scholarship as Jakob Grimm's *Deutsche Rechtsalterthümer* (1828). Not until Wilhelm Eduard Wilda's *Strafrecht der Germanen* (1842), which applied Grimm's methods of comparative philology to the treatments of legal violence in disparate Germanic societies, does the feud begin to loom over literary and legal-historical scholarship.[39] John Mitchell Kemble's *Saxons in England* (1846) was the first publication to acquaint English readers with the new interest in vengeance that was then beginning to agitate German historical scholarship. Kemble's comments on the feud introduce what would become a more or less permanent feature of scholarship on Anglo-Saxon England: namely, the vigorous defense of the feud's virtues as a means of social control:

> Where no *imperium* yet exists, society itself possesses only a *ius belli* against its own several members; and if neighbours

[37] See Francis Gummere, *A Handbook of Poetics, for students of English Verse* (Boston, Mass.: Ginn & Co., 1885), p. 176. An enlightening discussion of early views on Old English prosody can be found in E. G. Stanley, "The Scholarly Recovery of the Significance of Anglo-Saxon Records in Prose and Verse: a New Bibliography," p. 254.

[38] Klaeber, ed., *Beowulf,* p. 235.

[39] Wilhelm Eduard Wilda, *Das Strafrecht der Germanen* (Halle: C. A. Schwetschke und Sohn, 1842 repr. 1960), pp. 146-96 and *passim.*

will not be neighbourly, they must be coerced into peace (the great and first need of all society and the condition of its existence) by alliance of the many against the few, of the orderly and peaceful against the violent and the lawless.[40]

Kemble goes on to advocate the need of "Society" to "declare a war of extermination" against those who refuse to obey legal and social norms. Here Kemble's discussion of feud may perhaps be read as an indirect contribution to the contemporaneous debate over public executions.[41] Kemble's observations on the importance of vengeance to early Germanic dispute settlement certainly constitute a curious conflation of the ritualized violence of the feud with lethal punishments administered by the state.

From the middle of the nineteenth century onward, chapter 21 of Tacitus's *Germania* was cited as central evidence for the feud's status as a uniquely Germanic institution.[42] Particu-

---

[40] J. M. Kemble, *The Saxons in England*, 2 vols. (London: Taylor and Francis, 1849 repr. 1876), I, 268. A broad discussion of nineteenth-century efforts to re-imagine the Germanic-speaking peoples as "sturdy, freedom-loving, energetic" and "warlike" occurs in Peter Gay, *The Cultivation of Hatred* (New York: Norton, 1993), pp. 77-78.

[41] On the debate over public executions, see David Cooper, *The Lesson of the Scaffold* (Athens, Ohio: Ohio Univ. Press, 1974).

[42] "Suscipere tam inimicitias seu patris seu propinqui quam amicitias necesse est. nec implacabiles durant; luitur enim etiam homicidium certo armentorum ac pecorum numero recipitque satisfactionem universa domus, utiliter in publicum, quia periculosiores sunt inimicitiae iuxta libertatem" ("It is incumbent to take up a father's feuds or a kinsman's not less than his friendships; but such feuds do not continue unappeasable: even homicide is atoned for by a fixed number of cattle and sheep, and the whole family receives thereby satisfaction, to the public advantage; for feuds are more dangerous among a free people"). From Tacitus, *Germania*, p. 48; the translation is that of Sir William Peterson, trans., *Tacitus: Dialogus, Agricola, Germania*, Loeb Classical Library 35 (Cambridge, Mass.: Harvard Univ. Press, 1914 repr. 1946), p. 295.

lar emphasis was given to its observation that heirs receive the feuds (*inimicitias*) of their fathers along with their friendships. In support of the Germanic pedigree of heritable feuds, the immense commentary of Karl Müllenhoff adduces chapter 31 of the *Lex Thuringorum:* "Ad quemcumque hereditas terrae pervenerit, ad illum vestis bellica, id est lorica, et ultio proximi et solutio leudis debet pertinere" ("To whomever an inheritance of land should descend, he also should receive the battle-gear—that is to say, the breastplate—and the [obligations] of vengeance for kin and the payment of wergild").[43] Correspondences such as these are no longer as impressive as they earlier seemed, particularly since the *Leges Barbarorum* are now commonly understood in legal-historical scholarship as an amalgam of Germanic and Roman custom.[44] That the law of Rome also provided for the inheritance of a decedent's legal disputes certainly vitiates the authority of claims that there was anything uniquely Germanic about the hereditary descent of disputes.[45]

---

[43] See Karl Müllenhoff, *Die Germania des Tacitus erläutert,* Deutsche Altertumskunde IV (Berlin: Wiedmannsche Buchhandlung, 1900), p. 326; see also *Tacitus' Germania,* eds. Heinrich Schweizer-Sidler and Eduard Schwyzer (Halle an der Salle: Buchhandlung des Waisenhauses, 1923), p. 53. The latter, to be fair, does assert that the bloodfeud is an Indo-European phenomenon. The passage from the *Lex Thuringorum* is given in *Leges Saxonum et Lex Thuringorum,* ed. von Schwerin, p. 61 (chap. 27).

[44] See especially Ernst Levy, *West Roman Vulgar Law. The Law of Property,* Memoirs of the American Philosophical Society 29 (Philadelphia: American Philosophical Society, 1951).

[45] The archaic Roman law of the Twelve Tables likewise allowed for vengeance in cases of bodily injury where no agreement for compensation could be made; other injuries might be atoned for by fixed pecuniary penalties. The standard overview of these provisions remains that of H. F. Jolowicz, *Historical Introduction to the Study of Roman Law* (Cambridge: Cambridge Univ. Press, 1965), pp. 174-75. It is worth noting that Tacitus would almost certainly have recognized emendation of offences *certo armentorum ac pecorum numero* as similar to the customs contained in the Twelve Tables.

For example, Ulpian observes that in cases of offences to the dead the action on *iniuria* accrues to the inheritance and is thereby transmitted to the heir.[46]

Given its attestation in Tacitus, the feud became, like the communal ownership of land and the formulaic organization of legal utterances, a central criterion of archaism for nineteenth-century scholars. Acceptance of its imperatives was held to be indicative of "primitive," stateless and preliterate societies.[47]

[46] See Justinian's *Digest* 47.10.9.6: "Quotiens autem funeri testatoris uel cadaueri fit iniuria, si quidem post aditam hereditatem fiat, dicendum est heredi quodammodo factam (semper enim heredis interest defuncti existimationem purgare): quotiens autem ante aditam hereditatem, magis hereditati, et sic heredi per hereditatem adquiri" ("Now whenever there be any affront at the testator's funeral or to his corpse, if it occur after the inheritance has been accepted, it must be said that in a sense, the insult is to the heir (for it is always the heir's obligation to vindicate the reputation of the deceased); but if it be before acceptance, the insult is rather to the inheritance itself and it is thus through the inheritance that the heir will acquire the action"). Text and translation are from *The Digest of Justinian,* eds. and trans. Alan Watson *et al.* (Philadelphia: Univ. of Pennsylvania Press, 1985), pp. 771-72. See also William Warwick Buckland, *A Text-Book of Roman Law from Augustus to Justinian* (Cambridge: Cambridge Univ. Press, 1921), pp. 586-87.

[47] Wilda, for example, associates the feud with the state of nature: "Wenn es einen Naturzustand gäbe . . . so würde die Rache die herrschende, die einzig mögliche Form sein, in welcher das Recht sich Geltung verschaffen kann" ("Should there be a state of nature . . . then vengeance would be the dominant, the only possible form within which law might be enforced"); see *Strafrecht,* p. 157. Dame Bertha Phillpotts (*Kindred and Clan* [Cambridge: Cambridge Univ. Press, 1913], p. 6) also saw the feud as a survival of tribal society. Such views of the feud are rejected most recently by Patrick Wormald (*Making of English Law,* p. 26): "It is not too much to say that understanding of early medieval European law has now experienced a sea-change brought about by analysis of actual disputing. The justice of feud and settlement is no longer seen as a

The implied linear descent from feuding societies to those in which monarchs were invested with the responsibility for the punishment of crime was bolstered by popular evolutionary theory. Heinrich Brunner, the leading representative of the nineteenth-century *Rechtsschule,* shows himself to be susceptible to this preconception in a curious note from his discussion of the feud:

> Die Rache ist älter als die Rechtsordnung. Rechtliche und damit rechtsgeschichtliche Bedeutung erlangt sie erst durch die Stellung, die die Rechtsordnung zu ihr einnimmt, sei es an-erkennend, sei es verbietend. Ist das Tier älter als der Mensch, so ist auch die Rache älter als die Menschheit.[48]

> Vengeance is older than law. It obtains legal and thereby le-gal-historical meaning first through the position that the law adopts toward it, whether it be one of recognition or restric-tion. As the beast is older than the man, so is vengeance older than humanity.

It is well known that the labors of many nineteenth-century scholars on the Continent and elsewhere were devoted to re-covering the pre-Christian Germanic customs that ecclesiasti-

barbarous prelude to that of judgement and penalty but as a system with its own constructive logic. These perceptions have even been trained on the world of medieval Common Law. But this itself is a warning that resolution of disputes by mechanisms other than executive action does not preclude intervention by a powerful judicial apparatus with a political agenda of its own. That 'feud-centred' justice is most visible in relatively stateless societies does not mean that where it is visible there is no 'state.' It could be as mistaken to move over to a bloodfeud model of Old English justice, however sympathetically envisaged, as it would be wholly to substitute the rhythms of settlement for those of judgment in the thirteenth century."

[48] Heinrich Brunner, *Deutsche Rechtsgeschichte*, II, 223 n. 15.

cal culture had struggled to eradicate.[49] With a few exceptions (notably Levin Schücking), nineteenth-century students of *Beowulf* were also fiercely committed to an extraordinarily early date for the poem.[50] With the feud so firmly associated with primitivism, it is hardly surprising that scholars would argue for its presence in *Beowulf* where such an approach was not explicitly required.

The reception of the *Chanson de Roland* in the nineteenth and early twentieth centuries makes clear how much views of the feud could affect questions of dating and textual criticism. Léon Gautier was among the first to assert the Germanic origins of the *Chanson* in the late nineteenth century, and his arguments were based heavily on legal evidence.[51] Widespread acceptance of this and similar arguments ultimately made possible Ruggero Ruggieri's 1936 study, which contended that the trial of Ganelon shows features of a legal situation that would have been antiquated even in the age of Charlemagne.[52] The latter had attempted to eradicate the supposedly traditional right of vengeance, and since Ganelon claims in his defense to have planned the death of Roland in a state of feud, Ruggieri thought it likely that Ganelon was the hero of the poem in its earlier manifestations, and his execution a tragic demon-

---

[49] This aspect of nineteenth-century scholarship is explored in E. G. Stanley, *Imagining the Anglo-Saxon Past: The Search for Anglo-Saxon Paganism and the Anglo-Saxon Trial By Jury* (Woodbridge: D. S. Brewer, 2000).

[50] See especially Colin Chase, "Opinions on the Date of *Beowulf*, 1815-1980," in idem, ed., *The Dating of Beowulf*, pp. 3-8. James A. Harrison's view of the poem ("Old Teutonic Life in Beowulf," p. 16) was more or less typical: "The epic of Beowulf is a sort of poetic *Germania:* an unconscious poetic treatise on the customs and habits of the early Germans at once confirmatory of and supplementary to Tacitus."

[51] Léon Gautier, "L'Idée Politique dans les Chansons de Geste," *Revue de questions historiques* 8 (1868), pp. 79-114.

[52] Ruggero Ruggieri, *Il processo di Gano nella Chanson de Roland* (Florence: Sansini, 1936).

stration of the incipient conflict between local justice based in self-help and the expanding powers of the crown.[53] Emanuel Mickel's study of the trial rejects Ruggieri's thesis, finding no evidence for the view that feuding, however much it may have been tolerated in certain examples of royal legislation, was ever anything other than an extralegal means of dispute settlement.[54] Ruggieri and the adherents to his argument were also mistaken in assuming the feud to be an essentially archaic custom, as research in the twentieth century has adequately demonstrated its persistence throughout the Middle Ages.[55]

## THE SACRED DUTY OF REVENGE

That vengeance was a sacred duty and right of the ancient Germans is a major *topos* of nineteenth-century scholarship. All references to the "holiness" of vengeance are ultimately drawn from Wilda's *Strafrecht*, which was the first study of Germanic law to argue that the feud descends from an original "holy commitment of the Germanic peoples to blood vengeance."[56] Kemble likewise argues for a "right of private warfare . . . which every Teutonic freeman considered inalienable," one that "lies at the root of all

---

[53] See e.g. ll. 3758-60 (*La Chanson de Roland*, ed. Joseph Bédier [Paris: H. Piazza, 1924], p. 284): "Rollant me forfist en or e en aveir, / Pur que jo quis sa mort e sun destreit; / Mais traïson nule n'en i otrei" ("Roland did me harm with respect to my gold and possessions, and that is why I sought his death and his ruin; but I will not concede that there was any treason there").

[54] See especially the Introduction to Emanuel Mickel, *Ganelon, Treason, and the "Chanson de Roland"* (University Park: Pennsylvania State Univ. Press, 1989).

[55] See especially Hyams, "Feud in Medieval England;" Stephen D. White, "Feuding and Peace-Making in the Touraine Around the Year 1100," *Traditio* 42 (1986), pp. 195-263.

[56] ". . . heilig[e] . . . Verpflichtung der Germanen zur Blutrache." Wilda, *Strafrecht der Germanen*, p. 550.

Teutonic legislation."[57] Although Andreas Heusler does not characterize the feud as explicitly sacral, his *Strafrecht der Isländersagas* (1911)—a major influence on the work of William Ian Miller—shows its deep indebtedness to the tradition originated by Wilda in asserting the centrality of vengeance to Germanic life: "Vengeance can be a duty, the hardest, most demanding of obligations; above all, however, it is the desire and ornament of life."[58]

Belief in a "sacred" duty of vengeance among early historians passed without resistance into nineteenth-century literary scholarship, the major conduit being Vilhelm Grönbech's *Vor Folkeæt i Oldtiden*, translated in 1932 as *The Culture of the Teutons*. Lee Hollander's review of the first edition, published in 1910, was the first to translate for English readers Grönbech's insistence that one should "live one's self into . . . the characteristic ecstasy of the ancient Teuton," an ecstasy which occurs according to Grönbech "at the moment of accomplished revenge."[59] If Hollander was uncomfortable with Grönbech's assertion that the customs of the bloodfeud somehow constituted the very soul of Germanic civilization, subsequent scholarship rarely shared his reservations.[60] Grönbech's influence is palpable in Bertha Phillpotts's essay of 1924, in which she demands in similar language that students of *Beowulf* divest themselves of their civilized distaste for violence in order to understand the religious life of the early Germans:

[57] Kemble, *Saxons in England*, pp. 267-68.

[58] "Die Rache kann Pflicht sein, die härteste, anspruchsvollste der Pflichten; vor allem aber ist sie doch die Lust und Zierde des Lebens." Andreas Heusler, *Das Strafrecht der Isländersagas* (Leipzig: Duncker & Humblot, 1911), p. 48.

[59] Lee M. Hollander, "Review of Vilhelm Grönbech, *Vor Folkeæt i Oldtiden: I. Lykkemand og Niding,*" *JEGP* 9 (1910), pp. 269-78 at p. 272.

[60] "Unfortunately, Grönbech proceeds on the tacit assumption that the 'honor or vengeance' principle, as central feature in Germanic life, is unique. With this we are, of course, bound to disagree. Similar customs incident to similar conditions, have very commonly prevailed at all times among all races." Hollander, "Review," p. 274.

But if we are to understand the true force of those [narratives] in which vengeance plays a part, we must utterly rid ourselves of the haunting idea, natural to members of a policed society, that the pursuit of vengeance was a yielding to a passion, to a temptation. On the contrary; it was very often a deliberate sacrifice of wealth, happiness, even of personal honour, in order to fulfil an obligation which might be the holiest of all.[61]

The belief in an essentially Germanic duty of vengeance, along with an emphasis on its sacral character, was reiterated in 1938 by Hans Kuhn: "The duty of blood vengeance was clearly the highest and most sacred of all martial duties."[62]

As late as 1976, Bruce Moore claimed that Grendel's mother pursues her "sacred right of revenge" against the residents of Heorot, perhaps with more justice than Hengest's vengeance

[61] Dame Bertha S. Phillpotts, "Wyrd and Providence in Anglo-Saxon Thought," *Essays and Studies* 13 (1928), pp. 7-27, repr. in R. D. Fulk, ed., *Interpretations of Beowulf* (Bloomington: Indiana Univ. Press, 1991), pp. 1-13 at p. 3. Late nineteenth- and early twentieth-century students of *Beowulf* are often exhorted to adopt a kind of "mediumistic" approach to the poem: cf. Harrison, "Old Teutonic Life in Beowulf," 14: "In seeing exactly what the hero Beowulf saw, in trying to reconstruct for ourselves the life and landscape that surrounded him in the sixth century of our era (for one of the incidents in it has been traced to the year 511), we shall be getting a glimpse into the origins of our race . . . [W]e have but to look for an instant into ourselves, into our general Teutonic consciousness, and there we see its lineal descendants, the ideas which informed and moulded it. All things are in twilight, to be sure; but it is a dawn, not a dusk—it is the beginning of our Teutonic life, that we see pushing out vigorous germs, and striding towards the light with unmistakeable emphasis."

[62] "Die Pflicht der Blutrache ist offenbar das höchste und heiligste von allen kriegerischen Geboten gewesen." Hans Kuhn, "Kriegswesen und Seefahrt," in Hermann Schneider, ed., *Germanische Altertumskunde* (Munich: 1938 repr. 1951), pp. 98-122 at p. 218.

against Finn.[63] More recently, Hill has contended that the *Beowulf* poet's epithet for the sword placed in Hengest's lap by Hunlafing, *hildeleoman* ("battle-light"), connects the sword to the Germanic god Tiu, whom Hill takes to be "the ancient god of war as law, as settlement."[64] Hunlafing is thus read as asserting Hengest's religious duty of vengeance: "This, then, is the juridical sword of retribution, accepted world-wide (and originally having divine warrant) as an invitation to settle one's grievances."[65] Hill's observations make explicit the implications of earlier feud scholarship. References to vengeance as "a holy obligation" among the ancient Germans are, I suspect, deliberate inversions of the Christian emphasis on non-violence, and show the extent to which the feud has tended to become a vehicle for speculations on the nature of Germanic paganism.[66]

### The Nineteenth-century Legacy

That the duty of inflicting death on those who had wronged you became a "holy" thing in the minds of many nineteenth- and early twentieth-century scholars had concrete implications for the explication of the Finn Episode. R. A. Williams's 1924 discussion of *worold-ræden*, apparently the first to propose the now-standard interpretation of the compound, vividly demonstrates

---

[63] Bruce Moore, "The Relevance of the Finnsburh Episode," *JEGP* 75 (1976), pp. 317-29 at p. 328. Similar views may be found in Kevin Kiernan, "Grendel's Heroic Mother," *In Geardagum* 6 (1984), pp. 13-33.

[64] John M. Hill, "The Ethnopsychology of In-Law Feud and the Remaking of Group Identity in *Beowulf*: The Cases of Hengest and Ingeld," *PQ* 78 (1999), pp. 97-123 at p. 118.

[65] Hill, "Ethnopsychology of In-Law Feud," p. 118.

[66] G. F. Jones concludes that the belief in a sacred duty of vengeance among the early Germans "may have resulted from false analogy with Greek and Latin literature, in which revenge was often divinely inspired." See George Fenwick Jones, "Was Germanic *Blutrache* a Sacred Duty?", *Studia Neophilologica* 32 (1960), pp. 218-227 at p. 219.

the ways in which the dominant discourses of Germanist scholarship have imposed themselves on the interpretation of difficult terms. Williams's discussion begins with a concession (much like Klaeber's) that the various glosses offered for the term are scarcely reconcilable. He concludes that the meaning of the term "can only be found inductively with the aid of a hypothesis framed on our conception of the context."[67] The "context" is of course the world reconstructed in nineteenth-century scholarship, and once this has been supplied, the interpretation is easy:

> Hnæf's death left Hengest under an obligation to avenge him, which derived from the generally accepted opinion of his day that revenge was a holy duty for every man. This obligation was not removed but only suspended by the altogether exceptional necessity in which he found himself of giving pledges to Finn not to take revenge . . . Once, however, he had escaped from that situation by swearing fealty to Finn, revenge once more became a possibility, and the old obligation, for men of those days doubtless the most generally binding of all obligations, therefore became binding again.[68]

Williams was ultimately hesitant to go as far as Bolton and Wrenn do when the latter assert that MS *worold-ræden* can refer only to "the duty of revenge." His concession that the term is probably reducible to this definition is based exclusively on his belief that vengeance was the highest of Germanic duties.[69] Williams's most superficially persuasive argument for retention of the manuscript reading—the hypothesized similarity

---

[67] Robert Allan Williams, *The Finn Episode in* Beowulf: *An Essay in Interpretation* (Cambridge: Cambridge Univ. Press, 1924), p. 93.

[68] Williams, *Finn Episode*, pp. 94-95.

[69] "Now *worold-ræden* cannot mean 'duty of revenge,' but if this duty were felt in those days as the most generally binding, the one ranking above all others . . . it would be quite sufficient to refer to it as such because this could only imply one thing, revenge." Williams, *Finn Episode*, p. 95.

between *worold-ræden* and *folc-ræden*, "plebiscite"—is likewise not without major weaknesses. First, there was nothing new about the comparison of the two terms, which was initially suggested by Hermann Möller in 1883.[70] P. J. Cosijn found the original comparison erroneous:

> . . . *ræden* serves to help form abstract nouns which, if the main element has the sense of an action or the result of an action, differ but little from it: compare *gebed* and *gebedræden*, *(ge)cwide* and *gecwidræden* (*gecwedræden*), *treow* and *treow-ræden*, *camp* and *campræden*, *wig* and *wigræden*, *teona* and *teonræden*. *Mannræden* is "man" (collective as well), *hiwræden* and *husræden* are pure collectives of *mann* and *hiwa*.[71]

The notion that *ræden* here bears the sense of "decree" or "decision" thus suffers from serious difficulties. Even if the manuscript reading is to be maintained, it can hardly be said that the results add up indisputably to a meaning such as "decree of the world" or "universal practice," nor do these definitions, vague as they are, self-evidently amount to an injunction to vengeance.[72] Yet it is difficult to find in the literature on the Finn Episode any discussion of *woroldrædenne* that does not adduce, as the only means available of explicating this term, a hypothesized Germanic duty of vengeance.[73] This remains true even of

[70] Hermann Möller, *Das altenglische Volksepos in der ursprünglichen strophischen Form* (Kiel: Lipsius und Tischer, 1883), p. 68.

[71] P. J. Cosijn, *Aanteekeningen*, p. 20 n. 1142.

[72] North ("Tribal Loyalties," 25) suggests that with this term "the poet offers a poignant comment on the Danes' ensuing violence from the monastic point of view. Thereby he may also wish to contrast this bleak view of 'the world' with the 'worolde wynne' [joys of the world] (*Beo*, l. 1080) that were Hildeburh's before her brother and son lay dead before her."

[73] "To me it seems very probable that it may mean 'he did his worldly duty,' that is, the duty of revenge." W. W. Lawrence, "Beowulf and the Tragedy of Finnsburg," p. 418.

Brodeur's discussion of the term, the longest and most authoritative to date. Brodeur focuses his criticisms on Kemp Malone's claim that *woroldrædenne* might be a phonetic variant of *woroldrædende*.[74] While his arguments are indeed largely sound, it is difficult to see in them any conclusive refutation of Malone's and Klaeber's suggestions for emendation. Brodeur's lengthy battering of Malone's philological arguments ultimately amounts to a disappointing concession that *woroldrædenne*, should editors choose to emend it, "must be regarded, not as a legitimate phonetic variant, but as a scribal error."[75] For his contention that the compound should nonetheless not be emended, Brodeur invokes the Germanic love of the feud:

> [Hengest] stands apart from both his own Danes and from the Germanic view of a thane's proper duty. The Danes want vengeance above all things . . . To the *Beowulf* poet's audience vengeance undoubtedly seemed the better course. The heroic code demanded vengeance. Revenge for his slain lord, and that alone, could win general approbation for Hengest.[76]

It should be clear at this point how much the conventional interpretation of the Finn Episode depends on the assumption of a duty of vengeance among the Germanic peoples. Likewise, the assumption that Hengest is motivated by a duty of vengeance rests heavily on the interpretation of *woroldrædenne*. Belief in a Germanic duty of vengeance, along with a sense that this duty was in some way sacral or religious, probably contributed to the insistence in the early twentieth century on the tragic significance of the Finn Episode, inevitably accompanied by comparisons of Hengest to Hamlet, and of Hnæf to Hamlet's father:

---

[74] See Kemp Malone, "The Finn Episode in *Beowulf*," *JEGP* 25 (1926), pp. 157-172 at p. 159 n. 9.

[75] Brodeur, "Climax of the Finn Episode," p. 323.

[76] Brodeur, "Climax of the Finn Episode," pp. 329-30.

Hengest is in an acutely tragic situation; he is personally responsible for putting his followers and himself in the position of living on with the man who had murdered their lord. The conflict of duty is a nice one; torn between his oath to Finn and his duty to the dead Hnæf, with trouble likely to break out among the men at any moment, what are Hengest's emotions, what is he going to do? Here is a complication which demands unraveling. It is a perfect balance, of a sort dear to the temperament and traditions that gave birth to Hamlet. Is there not also, in some sense, a tragedy of Hengest?[77]

Ayres's reading is called into question by George Fenwick Jones's insistence that, compared with Latin and Greek literature, "Germanic literature . . . furnishes no parallel examples of vengeance taken at divine behest or for the satisfaction of the victim."[78] According to Jones, vengeance in the family sagas is above all "a matter of social prestige rather than holy duty."[79] That a legal duty of vengeance, explicitly sacral or not, ever obtained among the early Germanic peoples may itself be considered a highly suspect assumption. Among specialists in legal history, the notion that vengeance "lies at the root" of continental and Old Norse legislation has been seen as a proposition that at least requires significant qualifications. As early as 1871, Rudolf Sohm had argued that allowances for revenge in early Frankish law do not permit us to consider vengeance a right.[80] In support of this argument, Sohm cited a passage from Gregory of Tours's *Vitae Patrum* that bears repeating here. The narrative is concerned with a riot in Lyons in which a man slays another with a sword. The dead man's brother avenges him and is put in prison by a judge whose words, as reported by Gregory, unambiguously condemn

---

[77] Ayres, "Tragedy of Hengest," p. 290.

[78] Jones, "Was Germanic *Blutrache* a Sacred Duty?", p. 220.

[79] Jones, "Was Germanic *Blutrache* a Sacred Duty?", p. 227.

[80] Rudolf Sohm, *Die Fränkische Reichs und Gerichtsverfassung* (Weimar: H. Böhlau, 1871), p. 104 n. 5.

acts of vengeance: "Dignus est leto hic scelestus occumbere, qui voluntatis propriae arbitrio, nec spectato iudice, ausus est temere mortem fratris ulcisci" ("He is worthy of death, this wicked man who did not wait for the decision of the judge and who by his own will dared to avenge the death of his brother").[81]

By the early twentieth century the consensus of legal-historical scholarship had begun to turn away from the view that vengeance and the feud were sacred Germanic duties that enjoyed the full support of law. Franz Beyerle first argued in 1915 that what seem to be endorsements of feuding practices in continental legislation are best seen as indicating "resignation of the law, but not legal authorization of vengeance."[82] Julius Goebel lent his support to this view of the feud in his classic study of 1937:

> The feud is treated essentially as a troublesome state of fact . . . [R]esort to feud, while recognized as a means of dealing with wrongdoing, is never spoken of as a right. In other words, although it is not unlawful to resort to revenge, nevertheless, this resort is not had as of right, in the sense of a right recognized or confirmed by the laws themselves. The whole tendency and purpose of the folklaws of the Frankish empire is rather toward restricting bloodfeud, and furthering the process of emendation.[83]

---

[81] See *Gregorii Episcopi Turonensis Miracula et Opera Minora*, MGH Scriptores Rerum Merovingicarum I, ed. Bruno Krusch (Hanover: Hahnsche Buchhandlung, 1885), p. 247. I have retained the standard translation of Edward James, *Gregory of Tours: Lives of the Fathers* (Liverpool: Liverpool Univ. Press, 1985 repr. 1991), p. 58 (VIII.7).

[82] "Resignation der Rechtsordnung, nicht aber rechtliche Autorisierung der Rache." Franz Beyerle, *Das Entwicklungsproblem im germanischen Rechtsgang*, Deutschrechtliche Beiträge, Forschungen und Quellen zur Geschichte des deutschen Rechts, vol. 10, no. 2 (Heidelberg: Carl Winter, 1915), p. 42 n. 4.

[83] Julius Goebel, *Felony and Misdemeanour* (New York: Commonwealth Fund, 1937), pp. 18-20. Wormald (*Making of English Law*, p. 25) has judged Goebel's *Felony and Misdemeanour* to be "surely the twentieth century's best book in English on early medieval law."

The belief that the legislation of the continental Germans endorses feuding ignores the frequent expressions of abhorrence for its customs, usually encapsulated in attempts to limit the scope of the feud by shrinking the number of allowable targets for violence. The provisions of the *Lex Burgundionum* are fairly typical of this tendency, permitting violence against only the murderer himself:

> Hoc specialiter in huiusmodi causa universitas noverit observandum, ut interfecti parentes nullum nisi homicidam persequendum esse cognoscant, quia sicut criminosum iubemus extingui, ita nihil molestiae sustinere patimur innocentem.[84]

> This is to be observed everywhere in such cases, that the kin of the slain are to recognize no one but the killer as an object of vengeance, as we order him to be slain as a criminal; for we will countenance no harm to the innocent.

Provisions such as these could be mistaken as implying broad approval of vengeance, but analogous provisions of the *Lex Visigothorum* make clear that these measures were probably part of a general distaste for extralegal violence: "Quod ille solus culpabilis erit, qui culpanda conmiserit . . . Nec successores ut heredes pro factis parentum ullum periculum pertimescant" ("Let him alone be held culpable who committed the offense . . . Let not the successors or heirs fear any danger because of the deeds of the parents").[85] Lethal vengeance was an inevitable reality of early medieval society given its lack of policing, and while allowances for its existence could certainly be construed as tantamount to approval, it can no longer be argued that continental Germanic society authorized the feud whole-heartedly, or that the feud somehow expresses the peculiar "genius" of Germanic culture.

[84] R. de Salis, ed., *Leges Burgundionum*, p. 43 (2.7).
[85] *Lex Visigothorum*, MGH Leges Sectio I, ed. Karl Zeumer (Hanover: Hahnsche Buchhandlung, 1935), p. 256 (6.1.8 [Antiqua]).

In his extensive discussion of vengeance in Germanic legislation, H. Böttcher comes to similar conclusions about Scandinavian compilations such as the Icelandic *Grágás* and Norwegian Gulathing Law, both of which are routinely understood as displaying more acceptance of the feud as a means of dispute resolution than the *Leges Barbarorum*.[86] Even in these texts, Böttcher finds no evidence for a duty of revenge, nor of official endorsement of feuding practices.[87] Böttcher contends that assertions of the centrality of the feud to Germanic law are largely an effect of the methods employed by early legal historians such as Wilda, Konrad Maurer and Karl von Amira, all of whom aimed not to write the history of discrete Germanic legal traditions but to reconstruct from their remains an abstract "system" of Germanic law.[88] The result is that the boundaries between Frankish, Scandinavian and English treatments of the feud were

---

[86] "Ein Recht zur Rache oder besser: die Rache als rechtlich anerkanntes Institut kann allenfalls manchen Quellen im Norden entnommen werden" ("A law of vengeance or, better yet, vengeance as a legally recognized institution can possibly be discarded from many of the Norse sources"). H. Böttcher, "Blutrache," in Johannes Hoops *et al.*, eds., *Reallexikon der Germanischen Altertumskunde*, vol. III (Berlin: De Gruyter, 1978), p. 97.

[87] "Eine Pflicht zur Rache besteht nicht . . . Die Rachetat ist an sich nicht straffrei. Sie muß verkündigt werden (isl. *víglýsing*) und kann erst durch das Verfahren gegen den Toten straf- und bußlos werden" ("A duty of vengeance is not present . . . The deed of vengeance is not in itself free of penalties. It must be published and may only become free of penalties or monetary remedies after proceedings against the deceased"). Böttcher, "Blutrache," p. 96. Miller (*Bloodtaking and Peacemaking*, p. 238) likewise views Icelandic law as ultimately acting as a restraint to feud, in spite of what seem to be allowances for vengeance: "[P]eople took care to find adequate legal justification for their acts of revenge. They also planned with the knowledge that legally unjustified vengeance was liable to legal reprisal."

[88] See, for example, the Introduction to Brunner's *Deutsche Rechtsgeschichte*, I, 1-9.

blurred as historians grew to prefer a unified representation of Germanic feud customs—one which naturally privileged Old Norse sources for their dramatic content, as well as for their (according to prevailing assumptions) relative freedom from the taint of Roman and canon law.[89]

We have already seen that in the nineteenth and early twentieth centuries, philology was frequently envisioned as "[an] endeavor to relive the life of the past; to enter by the imagination into the spiritual experiences of all the historic protagonists of civilization in a given period and area of culture."[90] Accordingly, what unifies most early scholarly statements on the feud in Germanic literature is the desire to recover, often in ways that seem surprisingly emotive and subjective, pre-Christian and primitive states of consciousness, traces of which were held to be especially abundant in Old Norse texts.[91] Most statements discussed above on the nature of Germanic attitudes toward vengeance seem to confuse the willingness to countenance vengeance shown by some legislation with a widespread approval and even "love" of the feud among early Germanic-speaking peoples. This supposed affection of most Germanic peoples for the feud is, in turn, mentioned in order to highlight the extent to which their primitive sensibilities are remote from those of modern readers, accessible only through a deliberate suspension of the disdain for vengeance that is a condition of participa-

---

[89] This approach has been largely abandoned by legal historians; see especially Goebel, *Felony and Misdemeanour,* pp. 1-22; "Introduction," in Wendy Davies and Paul Fouracre, eds., *The Settlement of Disputes in Early Medieval Europe,* pp. 2-3; Patrick Wormald, *Making of English Law,* pp. 3-24.

[90] Cook, "The Province of English Philology," p. 1742. For a fuller discussion of this passage, drawn from Albert Cook's 1897 address to the Modern Language Association, see Introduction n.34.

[91] On the similar faith of early Chaucer scholarship in one's ability to divine Chaucer's intentions in moments of almost mystical insight see chapter 7 of David Matthews, *The Making of Middle English, 1765-1910,* Medieval Cultures 18 (Minneapolis: Univ. of Minnesota Press, 1999).

tion in modern civilization. What is curious about much *Beowulf* criticism of the late nineteenth and early twentieth centuries is its implication that such a suspension of civilized impulses is a desired outcome of scholarly work on early medieval texts; at the very least, a precondition to a proper understanding of early Germanic literature. Such statements no doubt reflect the attitudes of an era in which "primitive" peoples were held to be especially susceptible to ecstatic paroxysms of bloodlust (see chapter 4 for a full exposition of this subject).

What made the modern reader's recovery of such forms of consciousness possible were the "depth" models of identity that are among the hallmarks of modernism, and which then pervaded both popular and "scientific" psychology.[92] Common in this era is the assumption that primitive states of consciousness were "repressed" or otherwise submerged within an individual consciousness. These primitive attitudes might resurface under certain conditions, in the process offering moments of disorienting liberation to moderns who otherwise suffered under the weight of civilizing restraints. A buried inner primitivism was seen as the inheritance of all civilized persons, and philology occasionally offered itself as one of many means to its recovery.

Philologists were not the only ones living themselves into the "characteristic ecstasy" of the primitive worldview. In a 1928 essay by Zora Neale Hurston, the music of a jazz orchestra, like the violent rhythms of Germanic verse as characterized by Gummere, summons in a mediumistic fashion the primitive consciousness within, made known to Hurston through an overwhelming and irrational desire for violence. Hurston's essay is almost certainly an ironic allusion to the popular stereotype of the exotic primitive, but it can also be viewed as a burlesque of assumptions that permeated early twentieth-century thought:

[92] Paul Strohm, "Postmodernism and History," in idem, *Theory and the Premodern Text*, Medieval Cultures 26 (Minneapolis: Univ. of Minnesota Press, 2000), pp. 149-62 at p. 153.

> This orchestra grows rambunctious, rears on its hind legs until it
> breaks through to the jungle beyond. I follow those heathen—
> follow them exultingly. I dance wildly inside myself; I yell within,
> I whoop; I shake my assegai above my head, I hurl it true to the
> mark *yeeeeooww!* I am in the jungle and living in the jungle way
> . . . My pulse is throbbing like a war drum. I want to slaughter
> something—give pain, give death to what, I do not know.[93]

It is not unlikely that this former student of Franz Boas
(himself a forceful critic of the racialism that dominated early anthropology) is here responding to, if not satirizing, the
same assumptions that led generations of scholars to ascribe
crude motives such as the "love of feud" to what is perhaps
best understood as a celebrated Danish victory in battle. The
unrestrained rhetoric with which nineteenth and early twentieth-century scholars discussed Germanic attitudes toward
vengeance is surely one of the more peculiar results of a scholarly environment that aimed to use the remains of medieval
literature as a means of reconstructing archaic and "repressed"
forms of consciousness.

## CONCLUSION

It is significant that Klaeber's *Beowulf* refers most often for social
and legal information to works that were already antiquated by
time of the publication of the first edition in 1922. Klaeber alludes frequently in his notes to Grimm's *Rechtsalterthümer* and
Kemble's *Saxons in England*, but not at all to the work of their
successors—historians such as Brunner, Paul Vinogradoff, and
F. W. Maitland, whose major publications had been available for

---

[93] Zora Neale Hurston, "How It Feels to be Colored Me," *World Tomorrow*,
May 1928, repr. in *I Love Myself When I Am Laughing . . . : A Zora Neale
Hurston Reader*, ed. Alice Walker (Old Westbury, NY: Feminist Press,
1979), pp. 152-55 at p. 155.

two decades before his *Beowulf* went to print. His peculiar emphasis on early nineteenth-century historiography has caused contemporary *Beowulf* scholarship to rely on an understanding of the feud that is more characteristic of the nineteenth than the twentieth century.[94]

While the Finn Episode may indeed have something to tell us about feuding, it is worth remembering that our impulse to read the episode according to what is known of feud customs is an effect of the intellectual tradition within which *Beowulf* studies took shape, a tradition which especially prized examples of primitivism and paganism, and which was always anxious to point out the distinctly Germanic features of literary texts. There are few if any features of the Finn Episode that tie it unambiguously to other narratives of feuding. The importance given to the feud in interpretations of the Finn Episode seems to have been guaranteed by the status of vengeance as a peculiar fetish of early Germanist scholarship. Attempts by the scholars mentioned above to solve the difficulties of terms like *woroldrædenne* by means of the feud illustrate the dangers of assuming the poem's historical "context" to be anything other than the construct of a particular era of scholarship.

---

[94] For a sound overview of contemporary attitudes toward the bloodfeud and its importance to the history of Anglo-Saxon legislation see Alan Kennedy, "Feuds," in *The Blackwell Encyclopædia of Anglo-Saxon England*, pp. 182-93.

# IV

## *Feohleas Gefeoht:*
### ACCIDENTAL HOMICIDE AND THE HRETHEL EPISODE

BEFORE EMBARKING ON HIS FIGHT with the dragon, Beowulf pauses to remember in a lengthy speech the many
*guðræsa[s]* ("war-onsets") he had experienced in his youth.[1] The
first among them is no fight at all, but an accidental slaying he
witnessed while fostered in the household of king Hrethel: the
killing of Herebeald by his brother Hæthcyn, most likely in a
hunting accident. Though there is no question according to Beowulf that the fatal arrow was shot at Herebeald unintentionally,
Beowulf's statement that Hæthcyn "prepared a murder-bed"
(*morþorbed strêd*) for Herebeald suggests his reluctance to accept
Hæthcyn's blamelessness.[2] Beowulf later refers to the slaying of
Herebeald as a "feohleas gefeoht," a fight for which no monetary atonement was possible, and laments the fact that Herebeald necessarily had to die unavenged (*unwrecen*).[3] Toward the
conclusion of the episode, Beowulf again asserts the impossibility of any action against Hæthcyn:

> . . . wihte ne meahte
> on ðam feorhbonan   fæghðe gebetan;
> no ðy ær he þone heaðorinc   hatian ne meahte
> laðum dædum, þeah him leof ne wæs.[4]

---

[1] Klaeber, ed., *Beowulf,* l. 2426.

[2] Klaeber, ed., *Beowulf,* l. 2436. The neutrality of the term *morðor* should be
kept in mind: see chapter 3 p. 87 n. 30.

[3] Klaeber, ed., *Beowulf,* l. 2443.

[4] Klaeber, ed., *Beowulf,* ll. 2464-67.

He [Hrethel] could not at all seek compensation from the life-taker, not the sooner could he attack the warrior with violent deeds, though he [Hæthcyn] was not dear to him.

The rare compound *feohleas* has been interpreted as a legal term since the early nineteenth century.[5] To Benjamin Thorpe, one of the first modern editors of the poem, Beowulf's use of the term indicated that Hæthcyn's offense was "inexpiable with money."[6] That the deed could not be remedied by a pecuniary settlement led Thorpe to the conclusion that Hæthcyn's slaying of Herebeald was expiable only with blood. Such an attitude seemed uncharacteristically harsh to Thorpe and "at variance with what we know of the old German law, by which every crime had its price."[7] Thorpe's solution to the supposed discrepancy between Common Germanic practice and *Beowulf* was a naive suggestion that the penalty for accidental homicide contained in the Hrethel episode was a peculiarity of Swedish law.[8]

[5] The one other attestation of the term *feohleas* is not instructive. See the entry for 897 in Charles Plummer and John Earle, eds., *Two of the Saxon Chronicles Parallel*, I, 89. Plummer and Earle's edition remains the standard edition of the version of the *Chronicle* referred to by convention as E. The only other attestations of the term occur in manuscripts A (in the entry for 826), C, and D. See Janet Bately, ed., *MS A, The Anglo-Saxon Chronicle: A Collaborative Edition 3* (Cambridge: D. S. Brewer, 1986); Katherine O'Brien O'Keefe, ed., *MS C: The Anglo-Saxon Chronicle: A Collaborative Edition 5* (Cambridge: D. S. Brewer, 2000), and G. P. Cubbin, ed., *MS D, The Anglo-Saxon Chronicle: A Collaborative Edition 6* (Cambridge: D. S. Brewer, 1996).

[6] Benjamin Thorpe, ed., *Beowulf*, p. 164 n. 4873. About a decade before preparing his edition of *Beowulf*, Thorpe had completed what would be for some time the standard edition of the Old English laws, the *Ancient Laws and Institutes of England* (1840).

[7] Thorpe, *Beowulf*, p. 164 n. 4873.

[8] Ibid. His remarks about Swedish law indicate the extent to which the study of Anglo-Saxon law was still in its infancy.

Almost seventy years later, Klaeber adopted the gloss "not to be atoned for with money, inexpiable," and suggested that *feohleas* might best be understood as a synonym for the legal term *botleas* as it appears in Anglo-Saxon royal legislation.[9] Presumably Klaeber had in mind passages such as II Cnut 64, "Husbryce & bærnet & open þyfð & æbere morð æfter woruld-lage is botleas" ("Housebreaking and arson and thievery that has been discovered and flagrant homicide are without monetary compensation according to secular law"), where Liebermann glosses *botleas* as "unabbüssbar [durch Geld]."[10] The debt to Thorpe's earlier comments is clear: *feohleas* does not mean "without remedy" but "remedied only with death."[11] Less obvious (but perhaps more important) is Klaeber's debt to the great nineteenth-century legal historian Heinrich Brunner. Indeed, it might be said that the Hrethel episode is one of the few portions of *Beowulf* whose standard interpretation is ultimately derived from legal-historical and not literary studies. For there can be little doubt that Brunner's paper of 1890, "Über absichtslose Missethat im altdeutschen Strafrechte," remains the basis of all subsequent comment on the Hrethel digression. Its influence on Klaeber's conception of the episode, though probably indirect, is nonetheless evident in the latter's certainty that accidental homicide was punishable with death. Written in the heyday of the *Sakraltheorie* championed by his contemporary Karl von Amira—a hypothesis which held that in the earliest period Germanic death penalties were sacrifices meant to appease offended deities—Brunner's article uses the theory of sacral punishments to explain the *feohleas* nature of Herebeald's death, as well as to throw light on the connection between Beowulf's de-

---

[9] See the entry for *feohleas* in Klaeber's glossary (p. 328).

[10] II Cnut 64 (See Liebermann, ed., *Gesetze*, I, 352).

[11] As will be argued later in this chapter, Klaeber's reading also lends itself to the view that the term *feohleas* is employed in order to suggest that compensation could not be paid within the family. To my knowledge Klaeber never explicitly endorses either hypothesis.

scription of the slaying of Herebeald and the lurid account in ll. 2444-59 of an old *ceorl*'s grief upon the hanging of his son.[12] According to Brunner, the *ceorl* is in fact Hrethel, and the passage describes what would have been the fate of Hæthcyn had his father sought the appropriate punishment. The death of Herebeald had to remain *unwrecen* because it imposed on Hrethel an intolerable burden of vengeance:

> Einen hochtragischen Konflikt gewinnt aus der Strafbarkeit der ungewollten Tötung das angelsächsische Heldengedicht Beowulf. Von den drei Söhnen des Geatenkönigs Hrêðel hatte der zweite, Hæðcyn, das Unglück, seinen älteren Bruder durch einen Pfeilschuss zu töten, der das Ziel verfehlte. Das bereitet dem Vater schweren Harm. Denn der Tod des Edelings fordert Sühne. Aber zu grauenvoll dünkt es dem König, dass sein zweiter Sohn auf dem Galgen reite und den Raben zum Raub werde. In dieser Seelenqual wird Hrêðel trübsinnig und wählt den Tod. Nach der Auffassung des Gedichtes hatte Hæðcyn den Tod verdient. Er hatte mit Frevel gesündigt. Seine That galt für unsühnbar.[13]

The Anglo-Saxon heroic poem *Beowulf* gains a highly tragic conflict from the punishable nature of unintentional homicide. Of the three sons of the Geatish king Hrethel, the second, Hæthcyn, had the misfortune to slay his older brother by the shot of an arrow that missed the target. The situation brings bitter grief to the father. For the death of the prince demands expiation. But it

---

[12] Brunner argues for the sacral origins of vengeance in "Missethat," pp. 510-11. A comprehensive bibliography of the *Sakraltheorie* and its collapse appears in Kari Ellen Gade, "Hanging in Northern Law and Literature," *Maal og minne* (1985), pp. 1-2 ns. 1-5.

[13] "Über absichtslose Missethat im altdeutschen Strafrechte," *Sitzungsberichte der Berliner Akademie* (1890), pp. 817-42; repr. in idem, *Forschungen zur Geschichte des deutschen und französischen Rechtes* (Stuttgart: J. G. Cotta'schen Buchhandlung, 1894), pp. 487-523 at p. 489. The argument is repeated almost verbatim in Heinrich Brunner, *Deutsche Rechtsgeschichte*, I, 211-231.

seems too horrible to the king that his second son should ride on the gallows and become the booty of ravens. In this agony of the soul Hrethel becomes dejected and chooses death. In the view of the poem Hæthcyn had deserved death. He had offended grievously. His deed was regarded as without remedy.

The Hrethel episode was among Brunner's most important evidence for his larger argument that Germanic law is governed by a logic "which is blind to the situation of the individual case, closed to the existence of the criminal will."[14] Such a treatment of accidental wrongs corresponds to the "pantheistic worldview of Germanic heathendom," a worldview that was incapable of comprehending accident and which had no fully developed legal vocabulary for negligence.[15] According to Brunner the law of the *deodand*, a peculiarity of the English Common Law, also allows us to see the archaic formulation of liability for accidental wrongs from which modern practice has evolved.[16] The influence of Sir Edward Burnett Tylor's *Primitive Culture* (1874),

[14] ". . . welche blind ist gegen die Lage des einzelnen Falles, auf das Dasein des verbrecherischen Willens geschlossen." Brunner, "Missethat," p. 488.

[15] ". . . pantheistischen Weltanschauung des germanischen Heidentums." Brunner, "Missethat," p. 499.

[16] For a description, Brunner refers his readers to the following passage from Blackstone's *Commentaries*: "[I]f a horse, or ox, or other animal, of his own motion, kill as well an infant as an adult, or if a cart run over him, they shall in either case be forfeited as deodands; which is grounded upon this additional reason, that such misfortunes are in part owing to the negligence of the owner, and therefore he is properly punished by the forfeiture. A like punishment is in like cases inflicted by the mosaical law: 'if an ox gore a man that he die, the ox shall be stoned, and his flesh shall not be eaten.' And among the Athenians, whatever was the cause of a man's death, by falling upon him, was exterminated or cast out of the dominions of the republic . . . It matters not whether the owner were concerned in the killing or not; for if a man kills another with my sword, the sword is forfeited as an accursed thing." William Blackstone, *Commentaries*, I, 291.

a work known for popularizing notions of sociocultural evolution, is palpable in such claims. Tylor had himself attempted to explain the law of the *deodand* as a survival of periods in which the English were, like modern tribal peoples, held under the sway of primitive animism:

> The wild native of Brazil would bite the stone he stumbled over, or the arrow that had wounded him. Such a mental condition may be traced along the course of history, not merely in impulsive habit, but in formally enacted law. The rude Kukis of Southern Asia were very scrupulous in carrying out their simple law of vengeance, life for life; if a tiger killed a Kuki, his family were in disgrace till they had retaliated by killing and eating this tiger, or another; but further, if a man was killed by a fall from a tree, his relatives would take their revenge by cutting the tree down, and scattering it in chips. A modern king of Cochin-China, when one of his ships sailed badly, used to put it in the pillory as he would any other criminal . . . The spirit of this remarkable procedure reappears in the old English law (repealed in the present reign), whereby not only a beast that kills a man, but a cart-wheel that runs over him, or a tree that falls on him and kills him, is deodand, or given to God, i.e., forfeited and sold to the poor: as Bracton says, "Omnia quæ movent ad mortem sunt Deodanda."[17]

Opinion regarding the cultural significance of the *deodand* was not unified. In 1881 Oliver Wendell Holmes quoted this very passage, but did so in order to combat the notion that per-

---

[17] Sir Edward Burnett Tylor, *Primitive Culture. Researches into the Development of Mythology, Philosophy, Religion, Language, Art and Custom*, 2 vols. (Boston: Estes & Lauriat, 1874), I, 286. The same passage is partially quoted in Oliver Wendell Holmes, *The Common Law* (Cambridge, Mass.: Harvard Univ. Press, 1881 repr. 1963), p. 19. Brunner's citation of Holmes's text (see "Missethat," p. 518 n. 2) indicates that he would have been acquainted with Tylor's ideas whether or not he had read him directly.

sons were liable in archaic legal systems for accidental wrongs.[18] Holmes was unambiguously hostile to the theory as it was applied to Roman law, and probably would have felt similarly about Brunner's attempt to apply its premises to Germanic law:

> It has been thought that an inquiry into the internal condition of the defendant, his culpability or innocence, implies a refinement of juridical conception equally foreign to Rome before the Lex Aquilia, and to England when trespass took its shape. I do not know any very satisfactory evidence that a man was generally held liable either in Rome or England for the accidental consequences of his own act.[19]

The standard assumptions of nineteenth-century Germanist scholarship appear to have furnished Brunner with a means of avoiding Holmes's complaints. From models of *Rechtsschule* scholarship like Jakob Grimm's *Deutsche Rechtsalterthümer*, Brunner had inherited a methodology that allowed him to ignore the evidence of legislation when necessary, for authentic survivals of Germanic law were held to be present not in legislation but in literary evidence such as verse and proverbs. Such an interpretive strategy, in which proverbs and literature outweigh legislative evidence, forms the basis of Brunner's claims regarding the nature of accidental wrongs in Germanic society. His argument begins with a concession that liability for accidents does not survive intact into the era of literate law.[20] Fines, with or without surrender of the lethal object to the decedent's kin, are the standard remedies for accidental death and injury adopted in the legislation of all the Germanic peoples. According to Brunner, the introduction of Christianity and the intervention of monarchs in the settlement of disputes ultimately enfeebled the severe provisions that had supposedly obtained in

[18] Holmes, *Common Law*, p. 7.

[19] Holmes, *Common Law*, p. 7.

[20] Brunner, "Missethat," p. 490.

Germanic antiquity.[21] The somewhat convenient result of this development is that traces of the older, harsher treatment of accident are retained only in isolated statements in legislation (*vereinzelte Aussprüche der Rechtsquellen*) and in literature.[22]

Because it indicates a much harsher attitude toward accident than that attested by most extant legislation, Brunner had no doubt that much of the heroic and mythological literature of the Germanic-speaking peoples reflects "an archaic legal conviction of the people."[23] Though the Hrethel episode was crucial proof of Brunner's thesis, the central evidence for the legal archaism of Germanic literature came from its principal analogue, the narrative of Baldr's unintentional slaying by Höðr. The story is memorialized by three Old Norse sources, *Völuspá*, *Baldrs Draumar* and Snorri Sturluson's *Gylfaginning*. A garbled account also appears in Saxo Grammaticus's *Gesta Danorum* in which Höðr is a human who contends with Baldr for the affections of Nanna. In all four versions Óðinn, the father of Baldr, immediately sires a child named Váli (Bous in Saxo) who avenges Baldr.

For Brunner, the Baldr narrative illustrates unambiguously the nature of the archaic liability for accidental homicide:

> Dem Thäter fehlte nicht nur die böse Absicht, man wird nicht einmal von einer Fahrlässigkeit sprechen können, da den Asen, die Baldurs Unverwundbarkeit prüften, bekannt war, dass Frigg ihm von allen Wesen Sicherheit ausgewirkt habe und die Nichtverpflichtung der Mistel ihnen ein Geheimnis geblieben war. Nichtsdestoweniger gilt Hödurs That für eine solche, welche die Rache herausfordert.[24]

---

[21] Brunner, "Missethat," p. 511.

[22] Brunner, "Missethat," p. 490.

[23] ". . . eine uralte Rechtsüberzeugung des Volkes." Brunner, "Missethat," pp. 489-90.

[24] Brunner, "Missethat," p. 488.

> Not only was there an absence of evil intent on the part of the
> perpetrator; one cannot even speak of negligence, since it was
> known to the Æsir, who tested Baldr's invulnerability, that Frigg
> had obtained for him (Baldr) security from all beings, and the
> lack of commitment of the mistletoe had remained a secret to
> them. Nonetheless Höðr's deed counts as one for which ven-
> geance is required.

Brunner's reading of the Hrethel episode entered English
literary scholarship through a number of sources, the most
prominent being Francis Gummere's *Germanic Origins* (1892),
a survey of Germanic literatures that reiterates the Brunner hypothesis without alteration.[25]

A popular 1909 translation of *Beowulf* by the same author
makes similar claims in a note on the episode: "There is no
wergeld, says the poet, and revenge is out of the question. For
let one but fancy the feelings of a father who has caused his son
to be hanged!"[26]

W. J. Sedgefield's edition of 1910 appears to have been the
only scholarly edition of *Beowulf* in which the Brunner thesis
would appear without amendments.[27] Though the present consensus no longer reflects Brunner's view wholeheartedly, few
contemporary editions of *Beowulf* fail to repeat his assumption

---

[25] "[T]he poet of *Béowulf* seems to indicate that if the old king, Hrêthel,
had punished Hæthcyn in the way of the blood-feud for the innocent
murder of the elder brother Herebeald, it would have been by the
gallows. The monarch cannot bring himself to it." Francis Gummere,
*Germanic Origins,* p. 241.

[26] Francis Gummere, *The Oldest English Epic* (New York: MacMillan, 1909
repr. 1923), p. 127 n. 2.

[27] W. J. Sedgefield, ed., *Beowulf,* Publications of the University of
Manchester—English Series 11 (Manchester: Univ. of Manchester Press,
1910), p. 177 n. 2444.

that Germanic law recognized no distinction between accidental and deliberate homicides.[28]

LATER DEVELOPMENTS

Brunner's claim regarding the inability of early Germanic law to comprehend accidents appears to have engendered a number of enduring assumptions. In the century since his arguments were first published, only two significant modifications of Brunner's thesis were widely adopted, both of which also saw in the Hrethel episode a repository of Germanic legal norms scarcely attested in other sources. According to a 1913 doctoral dissertation by Arthur Bartels, it is not a crisis of conscience that keeps Hrethel from seeking vengeance, but his duty to abstain from violence against his own kin:

> Durch den Brudermord Hæthcyns war die rechtmäßige Fehde begrundet. Der Vater ist hier aber zwischen zwei Pflichten gestellt: als Vater und Oberhaupt des Geschlechts den Sohn und Sippengenossen zu schützen, und andererseits in gleichen Eigenschaften den getöteten Sohn zu rächen. In Gram und Kummer stirbt er, ohne Rache zu üben.[29]

> Through Hæthcyn's act of fratricide a condition of legally sanctioned feud obtained. However, here the father is placed between two duties: that of defending the (living) son and the kin group as father and chief of the family, and, on the other hand, that of acting in the same capacity to avenge the deceased son. He dies in sorrow and affliction, unable to perform vengeance.

---

[28] The pattern is evident in, for example, Daniel Donoghue's edition of Seamus Heaney's translation (*Beowulf: A Verse Translation* [New York: Norton, 2002]), p. 62 n. 3.

[29] Arthur Bartels, *Rechtsaltertümer in der angelsächsischen Dichtung* (Kiel: Chr. Donath, 1913), p. 105.

Bartels's study won the admiration of Klaeber, and probably would be forgotten had the latter not mentioned it in his bibliography on "Old Germanic Life."[30] Klaeber's bibliography also mentions a monograph of the following year by Johannes Müller that similarly abstracts from the inaction of Hrethel a rule of the Germanic bloodfeud: "Clearly Hrethel then would have the duty to avenge the dead Herebeald. But he cannot do so, for the killer is his [the deceased's] own brother and Hrethel's son."[31] Suggestions that Hrethel is restrained by pity from seeking vengeance seem to have ceased entirely after the first edition of Klaeber's *Beowulf*, whose note on the episode all but codified the earlier suggestions of scholars like Bartels and Müller: "Hreðel cannot fulfill the duty of avenging his son, because he must not lift his hand against his own kin."[32] In addition to the archaic liability for accidents, scholarship now saw an implicit rule of Germanic blood vengeance in the Hrethel episode. This rule in turn suggested to some scholars another way of reading Beowulf's assertion that the slaying of Herebeald was *feohleas*. The killing could not be remedied by money because a payment of wergeld could not take place within the kin group. In the words of the Donaldson translation, the slaying of Herebeald was not formally "inexpiable" so much as "without hope of recompense" since its resolution was a legal impossibility.[33]

The abandonment of one aspect of Brunner's reading ultimately engendered a new standard interpretation of the reference to hanging. Building on earlier suggestions by Rudolf Immelmann, Dorothy Whitelock argued that the gallows passage does not describe the hypothetical punishment of Hæthcyn, but is instead an extended simile likening Hrethel's legal position

---

[30] Klaeber, ed., *Beowulf,* pp. clxxvi-clxxx.

[31] "Hreþel hätte nun eigentlich die Pflicht, den Toten zu rächen. Aber er kann es nicht, da ja der Mörder dessen eigener Bruder und sein, Hreþels, Sohn ist." Johannes Müller, *Das Kulturbild des Beowulfepos*, p. 22.

[32] Klaeber, ed., *Beowulf,* p. 213 n. 2435.

[33] Tuso, ed., *Beowulf,* p. 43.

to that of an executed criminal's father.[34] Statements in Anglo-Saxon legislation prohibiting vengeance on behalf of executed criminals are the central evidence for Whitelock's reading. According to Whitelock, the gallows passage establishes an analogy between Hrethel and the father of a hanged thief, as the latter would have been explicitly prohibited from taking vengeance:

> It is natural that the author of *Beowulf,* describing Herebeald's fall, should call to mind the commonest type of *feohleas* death, and compare Hreðel's situation with that of a man whose son has suffered death as a lawbreaker. Just as effectively is he debarred from taking vengeance, just as terrible is his grief.[35]

The views expounded in Whitelock's brief article still command almost universal acceptance. Her arguments only intensified the consensus view that the Hrethel episode laments a tragic inadequacy of Anglo-Saxon (and presumably Germanic) legal procedure. As the Germanic law of homicide was configured solely in terms of the collective liability characteristic of the bloodfeud, Hrethel's duty to slay Hæthcyn (initiated by the latter's accidental slaying of Herebeald) was checked by his obligation to abstain from killing within the kin group. Similar claims were made in 1953 by Wrenn ("There could be no wergild, nor yet vengeance, as the king was the father of both slayer and slain") and Edward Irving in 1968 ("no wergeld can be taken and no vengeance can be exacted for the son's death").[36] Lawrence N. De Looze's important article of 1984 claims that the accidental killing of Herebeald was "an act for which ven-

---

[34] See R. Immelmann, *Forschungen zur altenglischen Poesie,* pp. 268-71.

[35] Dorothy Whitelock, "Beowulf 2444-2471," *Medium Ævum* 8 (1939), pp. 198-204 at p. 204.

[36] Wrenn and Bolton, eds., *Beowulf,* p. 188; Edward B. Irving, Jr., *A Reading of Beowulf* (New Haven: Yale Univ. Press, 1968), p. 224.

geance was both imperative and impossible to exact since subject and object of the murder were of the same family."[37] The most famous contemporary discussion of the Hrethel episode, a 1987 article by Linda Georgianna, contends that the episode "calls into question the coherence and meaning of the heroic world, which depends substantially on vengeance and fame to lend meaning to death."[38] Blame is again placed directly on the requirements of Germanic law: "King Hrethel, whose duty as the victim's kin is to exact vengeance or compensation from the killer's family, is also the killer's father. Thus there can be no avenging Herebeald's death and no resolving Hrethel's dilemma."[39]

Georgianna's reading of the episode exemplifies the tendency of much contemporary *Beowulf* scholarship to view the poem as an indictment of heroic values.[40] Behind such claims lies the shared conviction of many nineteenth-century legal historians that "archaic legal procedure was highly formalistic, tradition-bound and irrational compared with modern written law," a view that issues according to Clanchy from early anthropological studies and whose prestige has diminished greatly over the last several decades.[41] Here the habit of viewing Germanic insti-

---

[37] Lawrence N. De Looze, "Frame Narratives and Fictionalization: Beowulf as Narrator," *Texas Studies in Language and Literature* 26 (1984), pp. 145-56; repr. in *Interpretations of* Beowulf, ed. R. D. Fulk (Bloomington: Indiana University Press, 1991), pp. 242-250 at p. 245.

[38] Linda Georgianna, "King Hrethel's Sorrow and the Limits of Heroic Action in *Beowulf*," *Speculum* 62 (1987), pp. 829-850 at p. 837.

[39] Georgianna, "King Hrothel's Sorrow," p. 842.

[40] See especially E. G. Stanley, "Hæthenra Hyht in *Beowulf*," in Stanley Greenfield, ed., *Studies in Old English Literature in Honor of Arthur G. Brodeur* (Eugene, Oregon: Univ. of Oregon Press, 1963), pp. 136-51; idem, "Beowulf," in Peter Baker, ed., *The Beowulf Reader* (New York: Garland, 2000), pp. 3-34 at p. 31.

[41] Clanchy, "Remembering the Past and the Good Old Law," p. 171.

tutions as inflexible and irrational leads to the conclusion that the Hrethel episode constitutes a critique of these institutions.

## The Nature of Accident

Though the nearly unanimous support of *Beowulf* scholarship for the Brunner thesis caused his comments to be virtually ignored, at least one prominent historian seems to have doubted that Hæthcyn's offense should be interpreted as engendering a duty of vengeance on behalf of Herebeald. Frederic Seebohm called attention to the absence of a "necessity of flight or outlawry, however great the craving for avengement" following Herebeald's accidental death.[42] According to Seebohm, "[i]t is also significant that Hæthcyn, the slayer, is made to join with his brother Hygelac in the next warfare after Hrethel's death . . . [T]he accidental slayer remains a tribesman."[43] It is probably meaningful that Seebohm described vengeance as a "craving" in this particular case but not, as we might expect, a "duty." Later Seebohm states flatly that "[a]ccidental homicide does not seem to be followed even by exile," here taking Hrethel's inaction as evidence of his adherence to a legal norm.

Seebohm's arguments can potentially explain why Hrethel does not seek what most modern anthropological studies consider the standard punishment for intra-group slaying in feud societies: expulsion, often with lethal consequences for the slayer.[44] It is commonly understood that the Anglo-Saxon reflex of the exile custom is attested in Onela's response to the slaying of his nephew Eanmund by Weohstan—"no ymbe ða faehðe spræc, / þeah ðe he [i.e. Weohstan] his broðor bearn abredwade" ("He did not speak about the feud, though he had slain

---

[42] Frederic Seebohm, *Tribal Custom*, pp. 63-64.

[43] Seebohm, *Tribal Custom*, p. 64.

[44] See Jacob Black-Michaud, *Cohesive Force: Feud in the Mediterranean and the Middle East* (Oxford: Blackwell, 1975), p. 52 (though temporary exile was also possible, cf. p. 229).

his nephew").[45] As Seebohm first observed, the passage indicates that Eanmund "was a lawless exile, and so no longer entitled to protection from his kin."[46] That exile never seems a possibility throughout the Hrethel episode suggests that Herebeald's death, contrary to the opinion of most scholarship, may not have been perceived as tantamount to deliberate homicide.

It would seem that Seebohm's observations found no audience among twentieth-century Anglo-Saxonists. Klaeber, who otherwise made extensive use of Seebohm's *Tribal Custom,* ignored the latter's comments on the Hrethel episode, and all later scholarship appears to have followed Klaeber's example. In spite of some inevitable adjustments, there can be no doubt that Brunner's central claim regarding the nature of accident in Germanic law survives intact in contemporary *Beowulf* scholarship. The faith of *Beowulf* scholarship in the inability of Germanic law to distinguish between accidental and deliberate slayings has never faltered. In 1981, E. G. Stanley stated flatly that the "central concept of the [Hrethel] episode is the legal one of inexpiable crime," a statement with which no subsequent scholarship seems to disagree.[47] In the same article Stanley makes clear his position on the nature of accidental homicide in Germanic society: the Hrethel episode narrates an "unintentional and therefore inexpiable crime."[48] Generations of scholars have repeated Brunner's claim without undertaking any investigation of its merits. While it constitutes an admirable attempt to make sense of extremely taciturn and scanty evidence, I hope to demonstrate in the present chapter that a review of the underlying assumptions behind the standard reading of the Hrethel episode reveals that the present consensus may suffer from a number of insuperable difficulties. Therefore, Seebohm was

---

[45] *Beowulf,* ll. 2618-19.

[46] Seebohm, *Tribal Custom,* p. 67.

[47] E. G. Stanley, "The Scholarly Recovery of the Significance of Anglo-Saxon Records in Prose and Verse: a New Bibliography," p. 234.

[48] Stanley, "The Scholarly Recovery," p. 234.

probably correct to assume that it was the accidental nature of Hæthcyn's offense that spared him from any violent reprisals; indeed, there is a wealth of largely unexplored evidence in favor of this proposition.

The first point to be made against the Brunner thesis fortunately requires little elaboration. Brunner's explanation of why the death of Herebeald was considered inexpiable *(unsühnbar)* is based on a translation of "fyrenum gesyngad" (l. 2441a) as "mit Frevel gesündigt" ("criminally sinned"). This translation conflicts with the widely accepted reading first proposed by Klaeber, who repeated C. W. M. Grein's assertion that *fyrenum* is one of many instances in *Beowulf* in which the dative plural is used adverbially: thus *fyrenum* means "not 'wickedly,' 'with treachery'. . . but 'exceedingly,' 'greatly.'"[49] The Chambers-Wyatt edition repeats Klaeber's observation that the term is to be understood as an intensifier, the legal implication being that "no malicious intent is attributed to Hæthcyn."[50] E. Talbot Donaldson's standard translation of *fyrenum gesyngad*—"a deed wrongly done"—suggests the inapplicability of the notion of "crime" to the situation described in the Hrethel episode.[51] Brunner's assessment of the episode thus relies on questionable assumptions about a term that is key to the interpretation of the episode.

More serious problems—with more significant consequences for later scholarship—are to be found in Brunner's assumptions regarding the nature of the literary and legal texts that survive from the early Middle Ages. As was stated earlier, Brunner's essay is based on the conviction that heroic and mythological narratives, along with isolated passages in written legislation, often preserve the traces of preliterate and archaic law. Uncovering such traces was an undertaking whose results

---

[49] Fr. Klaeber, "Studies in the Textual Interpretation of *Beowulf*," *MP* 3 (1905), pp. 445-65 at p. 459.

[50] A. J. Wyatt and R. W. Chambers, *Beowulf with the Finnsburg Fragment* (Cambridge: Cambridge Univ. Press, 1952), p. 121 n. 2441.

[51] *Beowulf*, ed. Joseph F. Tuso (New York: Norton, 1975), p. 43.

were determined largely by the expectations of Brunner and his contemporaries. Nineteenth-century legal historians often employed implicit evolutionary models in their assessments of Germanic literature and legislation. For example, since the absence of a concept of property appeared to obtain among "primitive" peoples—in particular, the peasants of colonial India—it was held by scholars such as Sir Henry Maine to be a likely feature of Germanic tribal life as well.[52] (See chap. 2 for a more thorough discussion of the belief in primitive collectivism and its influence on textual cruces in *Beowulf*.) The widespread perception of a sacred imperative of vengeance was itself a criterion of archaism and primitivism (see chap. 3). As Brunner says in a different context: "As the beast is older than the man, so is vengeance older than humanity."[53] Since the various manifestations of the Baldr narrative seemed to complement standard assumptions regarding the processes of legal evolution, it was inevitable that these texts would be seen as more archaic and authentic exemplars of Germanic attitudes toward accident. Where Germanic legislation did not suit Brunner's expectations, the portions that did appear to be expressive of the archaic liability could be freely extracted from their context and regarded as independent traces of oral lawmaking.

Brunner's consequent emphasis on literary over legal evidence was an interpretive strategy licensed by the precepts of earlier studies by Jakob Grimm. The latter had argued as early as 1816 that literary and proverbial evidence was of equal if not greater interest to historians of Germanic law than legislative evidence, since verse and isolated legal proverbs were likely survivals of the oral tradition that preceded the introduction of Christianity and Roman law. (For a fuller account see chap. 1 of this study.) As such, they were scholars' only conduits toward

---

[52] See especially J. W. Burrow, "The 'Village Community' and the Uses of History in Late Nineteenth-Century England," pp. 255-284.

[53] "Ist das Tier älter als der Mensch, so ist auch die Rache älter als die Menschheit." See Brunner, *Deutsche Rechtsgeschichte,* II, 223 n. 115.

what was then the main object of legal-historical scholarship: the prehistoric and pre-Christian legal system of the continental *Germani*.

Traces of this element of Brunner's methodology are apparent in comments made by Whitelock—the only historian to overtly question aspects of Brunner's argument—when she notes the almost universal agreement among scholars

> that the accidental nature of the slaying would not in itself have saved the perpetrator from the penalties of homicide. *Qui inscienter peccat, scienter emendet, et qui brecht unge[w]aldes, betan ge[w]ealdes* says the post-Conquest compilation known as the *Leges Henrici Primi,* clearly embodying, and in part garbling, an Old English maxim. It is true that the same code only speaks of composition, not actual vengeance, for accidental homicide, but an incident in the life of St. Wulfstan of Worcester shows that as late as 1072-1095 the kinsmen might refuse compensation and insist on carrying on the blood-feud for an accidentally slain brother.[54]

A number of Whitelock's assumptions in the passage cited above may no longer be reliable. Certainly her reference to an incident from the *Vita* of St. Wulfstan of Rochester seems less compelling in light of more recent work on the bloodfeud. For some time it has been an axiom of modern bloodfeud studies that, as William Ian Miller writes, "settlements could be broken and often only postponed vengeance."[55] That the effort toward

---

[54] Whitelock, "Beowulf 2444-2471," p. 199. In the quoted passage Whitelock preserves the substitution of *þ* for *wynn* typical of many post-Conquest Old English manuscripts.

[55] Miller, "Choosing the Avenger," pp. 159-204 at p. 183. It is worth mentioning that the *Vita*'s account says nothing about whether or not the avenging party recognized the legitimacy of William the Bald's claim that he had killed their brother "casu non industria" ("by accident and not by design"): see *The Vita Wulfstani of William of Malmesbury,* ed. R. Darlington (London: Royal Historical Society, 1928), p. 38. As Emma Mason contends,

settlement mentioned by Whitelock should have collapsed may say less about the Anglo-Saxon treatment of accidental homicide than Whitelock indicates. As Black-Michaud argues, accidental homicide is a highly unstable category in most feud societies. Earlier attempts at pacification may easily be disrupted once the accidental nature of the initial slaying is forgotten or deliberately ignored:

> [W]hat may have initially been accepted as an accidental death can quite well blossom after a generation or two in the minds of the victim's kin into a deliberately gory atrocity seen as the first step in an eternal feud. Alternatively, if it is thought by the kinsmen of both the victim and the offender that the interests of both sides will be best served by mutual co-operation, the accidental nature of the death will be emphasized and the incident passed over with the minimum of commotion, though not forgotten.[56]

The very notion that the jural ideologies of tribal societies prescribe "absolute liability" for accidental wrongs—long one of the bedrock assumptions of anthropological study—is severely critiqued in a wide-ranging essay of 1994 by Laurence Goldman, who finds little to recommend further adherence to such a position. Goldman's essay is one of the few that attempts to historicize the assumption of "absolute liability," finding in this doctrine a self-serving attempt by early anthropologists to establish a safe distance between themselves and the objects of their study:

> [W]e glimpse here [in the doctrine of absolute liability] the familiar precept that defences of accident had to evolve or emerge, and on the basis of this chasm [between absolute liability and

the narrative certainly indicates that such a claim should ordinarily have resulted in a pecuniary settlement, and that the behavior of the brothers was regarded as aberrant both by St. Wulfstan and the community: see her *St. Wulfstan of Worcester c. 1008-1095* (Oxford: Blackwell, 1990), pp. 171-72.
[56] Black-Michaud, *Cohesive Force*, p. 19.

the Western doctrine of *mens rea*] the rigid dichotomy between Western and non-Western systems of thought was established. Moreover, legal anthropologists could feel confident in these evolutionary premises because they accorded with theories of misfortune generated elsewhere in the discipline; most notably in the fields of religion and comparative cognitive systems . . . [T]he position that legal anthropologists took on accident was merely acknowledging the time-honoured association of causality first with animism, and then with witchcraft. Traditionalistic thinking, it was held, sustained a single over-arching explanatory framework incapable of ideological conflict.[57]

Most significant for this study, however, is the atomizing approach adopted by Whitelock toward legislative evidence. In discussing the Old English maxim from the *Leges Henrici Primi* ("qui brecht ungewealdes, betan gewealdes") apart from its legislative context, Whitelock was almost certainly following the model of Brunner, who had likewise emphasized its centrality to the problem of accidental wrongs in Germanic law. The latter contends that while the author of the *Leges* recognized the appropriateness of the principle contained in the proverb, he was unwilling to follow its provisions to the letter, instead urging the application of *misericordia* by the king and his justices in cases of accidental homicide.[58] By mentioning the proverb, the *Leges* indicate that the archaic liability for accident was still tacitly recognized.[59] These arguments made their way into Pollock and Maitland's standard *History of English Law* (1898). Here Sir Frederick Pollock asserted that the proverb encapsulates "the principle of all Old Germanic laws" regarding negligence, and thought it comparable to a German proverb earlier mentioned

---

[57] Laurence Goldman, "Accident and Absolute Liability in Anthropology," in *Language and the Law,* ed. John Gibbons (London: Longman, 1994), pp. 51-99 at p. 62.

[58] Brunner, "Missethat," p. 495.

[59] Brunner, "Missethat," p. 495.

in Andreas Heusler's *Institutionen des deutschen Strafrechts*: "wer unwillig gethan muss willig zahlen" ("He who does [an offense] unwillingly must willingly pay compensation").[60]

Like Brunner, Whitelock seems to imply that the proverb preserves a more archaic understanding of liability for accidents than what appears in the *Leges*, one that required capital punishments. But throughout Old English legislation, including the early seventh-century code of Æthelberht, the verb *gebetan* is almost always associated with compensation rather than vengeance.[61] The German legal proverb mentioned by Pollock clearly refers to pecuniary settlement as well. If the custom of the prehistoric Germans considered vengeance the ideal response to accidental homicide, certainly the celebrated proverb does little to affirm the existence of such conditions.

### THE LEGISLATIVE BACKGROUND OF THE HRETHEL EPISODE

Whitelock's dependence on Brunner's methods attests to the extraordinary esteem in which his work was held until the latter half of the twentieth century, when legal historians such as Julius Goebel and, more recently, Patrick Wormald began to take issue with his use of legislative evidence.[62] Far less has been written about Brunner's use of literary evidence to bolster his claims

---

[60] See Frederick Pollock and Frederic William Maitland, *The History of English Law Before the Time of Edward I*, 2nd ed. (Cambridge: Cambridge Univ. Press, 1898), pp. 54-55. It is worth noting that the section of this work dealing with Anglo-Saxon law was authored exclusively by Pollock and left Maitland somewhat disappointed: see Patrick Wormald, "Frederic William Maitland and the Earliest English Law," *Law and History Review* 16 (1998), pp. 1-25; repr. in idem, *Legal Culture in the Early Medieval West* (London: Hambledon, 1999), pp. 45-70.

[61] Whitelock makes this very point earlier in the article: see her "Beowulf 2444-2471," p. 201 n. 5.

[62] Goebel, *Felony and Misdemeanor*, chapter 1; Wormald, *Making of English Law*, pp. 11-14.

about legislation. By Brunner's own admission, legislative traces of the archaic principle of liability are scarce. Its presence is suggested solely by obscure allusions, or by practices which were introduced to supplant it. The only legislative evidence by which Brunner attempts to substantiate his claims regarding the legal underpinnings of the Hrethel episode is drawn from chapter 19 of the *Lex Baiwariorum*. The remedies proposed in that chapter for the defamation of corpses make clear, according to Brunner, "that in Bavarian law" and thus, presumably, Germanic law itself, "the case of accident was handled in a manner identical to that of an intentional action."[63] Brunner mentions two cases: one in which a man has decapitated or otherwise mutilated the corpse of a man whom someone else had slain, and another in which a man, while attempting to shoot at carrion birds as they devour a corpse, unintentionally shoots the corpse.[64] For both cases the Bavarian code prescribes a fine of twelve *solidi* to the kin of the deceased. The identical compensation amounts were clear evidence to Brunner

> daß ungewollte Tat nach uralter Rechtsüberzeugung des Volkes als gewollte Missetat zugerechnet und gebüßt, daß beispielsweise die Tötung oder Verwundung, die ein abirrender Pfeil verursachte, gleich der absichtlichen Tötung oder Verwundung geahndet wurde.[65]

> . . . that according to an ancient legal conviction of the people an unintentional deed was reckoned intentional and compensated for as such, that for example death or wounding originating from an errant arrow was punished like deliberate killing or wounding.

[63] ". . . dass im bayrischen Rechte . . . der Fall der Abirrung gleich der gewollten Tat behandelt wurde." Brunner, "Missethat," p. 491.

[64] *Lex Baiwariorum,* MGH Legum Sectio I vol. V, ed. Ernst von Schwind (Hanover: Hahnsche Buchhandlung, 1926), pp. 456-57.

[65] Brunner, *Deutsche Rechtsgeschichte,* II, 715.

It is important to keep in mind that Brunner mentions this passage in connection with the Hrethel episode. His argument clearly conflates requirements for wergeld payments with requirements for vengeance, and what makes such a conflation possible is presumably the evolutionary master-narrative underlying much legal-historical scholarship of the nineteenth-century in which harsher provisions of the law precede milder ones. We can see a similar logic in Klaeber's observation that "[a]ccidental homicide was punishable," a remark that precedes comments on Hrethel's duty of vengeance.[66] Like Brunner, Klaeber appears to have felt that because accidental homicide was everywhere punishable with fines, it was unnecessary to furnish proof of the claim that it had earlier been punishable with death. Injunctions to make wergeld payments were viewed as the shadows of earlier death penalties.

At least where pecuniary settlements were concerned, Germanic legislators probably were not overly concerned with whether a wrong was accidental or intended. In this sense alone, Brunner may have been right. In the most general sense, both accidental and deliberate offenses might provoke vengeance. But outside of the Baldr myth, there is little if any evidence to the effect that this vengeance might take place without the avenging party having first refused to see the offense as accidental. And as Miller has argued, the willingness of the offender to pay a fine was the principal means by which he established the absence of his intent.[67] Hence the imposition of fines for accidental harm in the *Leges Barbarorum* is less likely to be punitive (as Brunner and Klaeber suggest) than precautionary.

The evidence of the earliest Lombard laws is a case in point. As Wormald has recently observed, no continental legislation is

---

[66] Klaeber, ed., *Beowulf,* p. 213 n. 2435.

[67] Miller adduces evidence from *Grágás* indicating that only in the absence of prompt amends for damage was an offense assumed not to be an accident: see Miller, *Bloodtaking and Peacemaking,* p. 62.

as lenient as Rothair's edict in its allowances for the bloodfeud. Among all the *Leges Barbarorum*, the edict evinces in a way that other codes do not what earlier scholarship might have called a "thoroughly Germanic character." Wormald's comments on this subject are authoritative and worth quoting *in extenso*:

> Whereas Visigothic law excluded the liability of kindreds for anyone's crime, Rothari went on to record as increasing the sums due for injury "that feud be deferred (*ut faida postponatur*)." He thus accepted the answerability of a kingroup for what its members did, only hoping that adequate compensation would avoid further violence. Feud remained central to his vision of law and order. Feud was not a process known or acceptable to Roman law . . . It follows that Rothari must be taken seriously when claiming to have drawn on "the ancient law of the Lombards."[68]

Given its generally accepted adherence to Lombard custom, we should certainly expect to see some trace of the archaic liability for accident in a text like Rothair's edict. Yet in all cases of accidental homicide, the response of Rothair is to suggest compensation, "cessante faida, eo quod nolendo fecerunt" ("the feud ceasing, since they did [the offense] unwillingly").[69] If Rothair can almost unfailingly be understood as codifying Germanic custom, it is fair to ask why the archaic liability for accidents is wholly absent in his edict—particularly when Brunner was able to draw on it for evidence of ancient sacral executions.[70]

It may be instructive to consider another celebrated proof of the old Germanic liability for accidents, chapter 18 of the *Lex*

---

[68] Wormald, *Making of English Law*, p. 39.

[69] *Leges Langobardorum*, MGH Legum Sectio I vol. IV (Hanover: Hahnsche Buchhandlung, 1869), chapter 75 (p. 24). The phrase is repeated in chapter 138 (p. 32): ". . . cessante faida, ideo quia nolendo fecerunt."

[70] See Brunner, "Missethat," pp. 510-11, where he notes traces in Rothair's legislation of the ancient Germanic *Opfertod* or sacral execution.

*Burgundionum.* Though the chapter explicitly repeals penalties
for accidental injury and death, its opening statement alludes
to early provisions that had obtained among the non-Roman
population of Burgundy:

> Si quodcumque animal quolibet casu aut morsus canis homini
> mortem intulerit, iubemus etiam inter Burgundiones antiquam
> exinde calumniam removeri, quia quod casus operatur non de-
> bet ad damnum aut inquietudinem hominis pertenire  [. . .]
> Lancea vero vel quodcumque genus armorum aut proiectum
> in terra aut fixum simpliciter fuerit et casu se ibidem homo aut
> animal inpulerit, illum cuius arma fuerit, nihil iubemus exsol-
> vere, nisi forte sic arme in manu teneat, ut homini periculum
> possit inferre.[71]

> If any animal by chance, or if any dog by bite, causes death
> to a man, we order that among Burgundians the ancient rule
> of blame be removed henceforth: because what happens by
> chance ought not to conduce to the loss or discomfiture of
> man. [. . .] In truth, if a lance or any kind of weapon shall have
> been thrown upon the ground and set there without intent to
> do harm (*simpliciter*), and if by accident a man or animal im-

---

[71] R. de Salis, ed., *Leges Burgundionum,* pp. 56-57; trans. Katherine Fischer
Drew, *The Burgundian Code* (Philadelphia: Univ. of Pennsylvania Press,
1949 repr. 1976), p. 35. The omitted passage requires that, should a horse
bite a horse or a dog another dog, the offending animal must be handed
over to the owner of the injured animal. De Salis refers his readers to
Brunner's "Missethat" for an explanation of chapter 18, where the latter
maintains that requirements such as these resemble the vengeance taken
by tribal peoples upon animals or falling trees. It seems more likely that
such requirements are simply a means of restitution, indemnifying the
owner of the injured animal for the value of his loss. Provisions like these
have nothing in common with the law of the *deodand* (which was, as
Blackstone indicates, above all a means of raising revenue for the royal
household).

pales himself thereupon, we order that he to whom the weapon belongs shall pay nothing unless by chance he held the weapon in his own hands in such a manner that it could cause harm to a man.

It was inevitable that references to an "ancient rule of blame" in the *Lex Burgundionum* would cause Germanist scholars to prick up their ears. The first to offer any significant comment on the chapter was a French disciple of Jakob Grimm, Garabed Davoud-Oghlou, who suggested in 1845 that the *antiqua calumnia* is probably one of the many Latin synonyms in the *Leges Barbarorum* for *faida* or "feud." On this basis, Davoud-Oghlou argued that according to chapter 18 "the feud is entirely forbidden for all involuntary wrongs."[72] His arguments survive unchanged in Katherine Fischer-Drew's standard translation of the code: "Perhaps this is a reference to the early Germanic *faida* or law of revenge, for our law here seems to imply that under the 'ancient rule of blame' a man was held personally accountable for the actions of his animals."[73] As Fischer-Drew's note makes clear, by interpreting *antiqua calumnia* as synonymous with *faida,* scholarship has consistently assumed that the *Lex Burgundionum* is here repealing earlier requirements for vengeance. But the *Lex* is not repealing a right of the injured party to pursue vengeance. It is repealing the right to composition—"nihil iubemus exsolvere" ("we prescribe no payment"). There is every reason to believe that it is the expectation of a pecuniary settlement that is contained in the phrase *antiqua calumnia,* and not the right of vengeance.

Further scrutiny of the text that lies at the root of contemporary views of the Hrethel episode—the *Leges Henrici Primi*—offers

---

[72] ". . . [l]a faida est entièrement interdite pour tout dommage involuntaire." Garabed Artin Davoud-Oghlou, *Histoire de la législation des anciens germains,* 2 vols. (Berlin: G. Reimer, 1845), I, 399.

[73] Drew, *Burgundian Code,* p. 35 n. 1.

little encouragement for the view that accidental and deliberate offenses were treated identically in early Germanic law. As the *Leges* make clear, in some cases of accident even the imposition of fines was viewed as excessive. The text begins its discussion of homicide with the following quotation from St. Augustine's *De sermone Domini in monte*:

> Si homicidium est hominem occidere, potest aliquando accidere sine peccato, nam miles hostem et iudex nocentem et cui forte inuito uel inprudenti telum manu fugit, non michi uidentur peccare cum hominem occidunt.[74]

> If homicide is killing a man, it can sometimes happen without committing sin; for a soldier who kills his enemy, and a judge a criminal, and a person from whose hand a spear flies perhaps involuntarily or accidentally, do not seem to me to commit a sin when they kill a man.

According to the *Leges* there had never been a time when accidental homicide had necessarily engendered a legally sanctioned liability beyond requirements to pay compensation. In at least one case, the author of the *Leges* finds even demands for compensation preposterous:

> Si homo cadat ab arbore uel quolibet mechanico super aliquem ut inde moriatur uel debilitetur, si certificare ualeat quod amplius non potuit, antiquis institutionibus habeatur innoxius. Vel si quis obstinata mente contra omnium estimationem uindicare uel weram exigere presumpserit, si placet, ascendat et illum similiter obruat.[75]

---

[74] See *Leges Henrici Primi*, ed. and trans. L. J. Downer (Oxford: Clarendon, 1972), chapter 72 Ic (pp. 228-29).

[75] *Leges Henrici Primi*, ed. and trans. L. J. Downer, chapters 90, 7-7a (pp. 282-83).

> If a man falls from a tree or some man-made structure on to
> someone else so that as a result the latter dies or is injured, if
> he can prove that he was unable to avoid this, he shall in accor-
> dance with ancient ordinances be held blameless.
> Or if anyone stubbornly and against the opinion of all takes it
> upon himself to exact vengeance or demand wergeld, he shall
> if he wishes climb up and in similar fashion cast himself down
> on the person responsible.

In spite of its derisive attitude toward vengeance for accidents, Brunner believed that the passage cited above indicates
the persistence of a more traditional attitude toward accident
in its very attempt to subvert it: "The extremely stringent application of the talion is meant to lead *ad absurdum* the severe
law which once gave to the kin of the deceased the authority to
perform blood vengeance or to demand *wergeld*."[76]

But the compilator's assertion that in such accidents the sur-
vivor is blameless according to ancient ordinances (*antiquis in-
stitutionibus*), combined with his claim that one who sought vengeance or compensation for the decedent would be doing so
obstinately and against universal opinions (*obstinata mente contra
omnium estimationem*), is evidence that provisions of the law ob-
viating the need for vengeance in cases of accidental homicide
need not be seen as the result of ecclesiastical and royal inter-
ventions. According to the compiler of the *Leges*, vengeance for
accidental homicide might be prohibited by both custom and
ancient tradition.

Provisions on accident in the Scandinavian legal compilation
known as *Jónsbók*, promulgated in 1281 but based in part on
traditional Norwegian law, are further evidence for the leniency
of Germanic law in cases of accident. The text also offers an in-

[76] "Die peinlich genaue Anwendung der Talion soll das strenge Recht ad
absurdum führen, welches einst der Sippe des Getöteten die Befugnis
gab, Blutrache zu üben oder das Wergeld zu beanspruchen." Brunner,
"Missethat," p. 493.

teresting basis of comparison for the rare compound *feohleas* to which Klaeber attached so much importance:

> Þar sem maðr tekr manni blóð, eða leggr eld á mann, eða þat annat með lækningu, er hvárr tveggi hyggr heilsubót af verða, þá er þat með öllu bótalaust, þó at hinni fái bana eða mein af.[77]

> Where a man takes blood from a man, or places fire on a man, or attempts to heal him with medicine from which each of the two expects an improvement in health to result, then is that [action] entirely without *bót*, although one has received death or injury from it.

Here the cognate compound *bótalaust* can only mean "not to be remedied with money, free of legal penalties." A similar principle emerges from the Icelandic compilation *Grágás*. The famous line with which it introduces the discussion of accident—"Þat er mælt, at engi skulu vera váðaverk" ("It is declared that there shall be no accidents")—might easily lend itself to the view endorsed by Brunner.[78] But as Miller argues, this statement did not indicate "that in matters of doubt a wrong should be deemed intentional. It simply means that accidents are not to provide a basis for a cause of action. The claim of accident is a defense to an action for an intentional wrong."[79] Such a principle was not alien to Anglo-Saxon legislation. Perhaps most intriguing is the statement of II Cnut 68.3, a revision of the Old English proverb that received so much attention in the late

---

[77] See *Jónsbók. Kong Magnus Hakonssons Lovbog for Island*, ed. Ólafur Halldórsson (Odense: Odense Universitetsforlag, 1970), chapter 13 (p. 49).

[78] *Grágás efter det Anamagnæanske Haandskrift Nr. 334 fol., Staðarhólsbók*, ed. Vilhjálmur Finsen (Copenhagen: Gyldendalske Boghandel, 1879), chapter 296 (p. 334).

[79] Miller, *Bloodtaking*, pp. 65-66.

nineteenth century: "[G]if hwa ungewealdes deð, ne byð þæt eallunga gelic ðam, ðe hit gewealdes deð" ("[I]f anyone acts unintentionally, he is not entirely like one who does it intentionally").[80] While it is worth mentioning that this axiom reflects the standard view of Anglo-Saxon penitentials toward unintentional wrongs, and that Cnut's code was composed by Archbishop Wulfstan, we should recall that both Brunner and Whitelock did not hesitate to mine Cnut's legislation for survivals of old Germanic custom.[81] Moreover, establishing the indebtedness of such statements to penitential literature does not necessarily diminish their value as evidence by which to reconstruct the handling of unintentional wrongs among Germanic-speaking peoples. In an influential essay of 1995, Thomas Charles-Edwards argued that the penitential attributed to Archbishop Theodore (and hence the many that are derived from it) is best seen as making concessions "to the conditions of a country in which feud was part of the fabric of society."[82]

Such views complicate the opposition of Christian and pre-Christian institutions upon which so much nineteenth-century

---

[80] For the standard text of II Cn. 68.3 see Liebermann, ed., *Gesetze,* I, 354-55; trans. Whitelock, ed., *EHD,* p. 428. See also Roger Fowler, "A Late Old English Handbook for the Use of a Confessor," *Anglia* 83 (1965), pp. 1-34 at pp. 17-34.

[81] See especially Whitelock, "Beowulf 244-2471," p. 203. The penitential attributed to Bede, for example, prescribes one year of penance for accidental slaying as opposed to four years of penance for deliberate slaying. Such provisions are typical of Anglo-Saxon penitentials. For a fuller discussion see Allen Frantzen, *The Literature of Penance in Anglo-Saxon England* (New Brunswick: Rutgers Univ. Press, 1983), p. 7.

[82] See Thomas Charles-Edwards, "The Penitential of Theodore and the *Iudicia Theodori,*" in *Archbishop Theodore: Commemorative Studies on his Life and Influence,* Cambridge Studies in Anglo-Saxon England 11, ed. Michael Lapidge (Cambridge: Cambridge Univ. Press, 1995), pp. 141-174 at p. 170.

scholarship depended. For Brunner and his followers, to establish the Christian pedigree of a given practice was sufficient to nullify its usefulness. Indeed, the hunt for survivals of the archaic liability for accidental wrongs often has a disturbingly indiscriminate quality in early legal-historical scholarship, the only criteria of archaism being what institutional conventions required one to expect at various points of the more or less uniform legal development that all societies were held to have undergone.

Ultimately there is little if any evidence that the Germanic liability for accidents ever required more than a pecuniary settlement. It is probably significant that Brunner's discussion of accident in his *Deutsche Rechtsgeschichte,* which otherwise reproduces his 1890 article word for word, drops earlier allusions to *Sigurðarkviða Fáfnisbana* (whose standard title is now *Reginsmál*) while retaining references to *Beowulf* and the Baldr myth. According to Brunner's own assumptions regarding the evolution of law, literary and mythological evidence should endorse vengeance in place of compensation where accidental homicide is concerned. Yet in *Sigurðarkviða Fáfnisbana,* Hreiðmarr requests a monetary settlement to redeem the life of Loki, who had slain an otter at the urging of the other Æsir without knowing that Hreiðmarr's son had assumed the animal's form.[83]

Because of its supposed proximity—at least in sentiment and worldview—to Germanic antiquity, Brunner was willing to give literary evidence an importance that it may not have deserved, even while he ignored the often contradictory nature of literary statements on accident.

---

[83] Brunner's observations are based on *Sæmundar Edda hins fróða,* ed. Sophus Bugge (Christiania: P. T. Mallings Forlagsboghandel, 1867), pp. 212-16. The standard edition is Gustav Neckel, ed., *Edda: Die Lieder des Codex Regius nebst verwandten Denkmälern,* 5th cd., rev. Hans Kuhn (Heidelberg: C. Winter, 1983), pp. 173-9.

## CONCLUDING REMARKS

Given that the defense of accidental homicide might well have spared Hæthcyn's life after all, we may wonder how much authority should be granted to the standard claim that Hrethel refrains from vengeance due to the bonds of kinship alone. Reasons for doubt may issue from the most celebrated literary analogue of the Hrethel episode. In all of its forms, the Baldr narrative is ostensibly a fulsome endorsement of the very practice that was, according to the dominant view, forbidden Hrethel by the imperatives of Germanic custom.[84] De Looze remains the only scholar to comment (though only dismissively) on how the vengeance enacted by Váli might complicate standard assumptions about the Hrethel episode. While Óðinn may have avenged his son through a surrogate, for Hrethel

> this course of action is hardly feasible, since ordinary human beings cannot count on their progeny doing battle at such a tender age and, more important, because even if one son were avenged in this fashion murderer and murdered would still be within the same family.[85]

De Looze's observations are somewhat unsatisfying in that they do not address the question why vengeance within the kin should ostensibly be permitted in the Baldr narrative and not in the Hrethel episode. At least one scholar attempts to solve this problem by proposing that the Baldr narrative mentions intra-group vengeance only to condemn it. According to John Lindow, what compels us to see Óðinn's reprisal against Höðr negatively is the characteristically Germanic abhorrence

---

[84] But see the caveats against such a comparison in Klaeber, ed., *Beowulf,* p. xli; R. D. Fulk, "An Eddic Analogue to the Scyld Scefing Story," *RES* n.s. XL (1989), pp. 313-322 at p. 322 n. 31.

[85] De Looze, "Beowulf as Narrator," p. 247 n. 8.

for intra-group vengeance. His principal evidence for such a prohibition is Beowulf's allusion to Unferð's kin-slaying, for which the latter "in helle scea[l]//werhðo dreogan" ("shall suffer damnation in hell").[86] Lindow's reading also depends significantly on the standard view of the Hrethel episode for proof of the Germanic rule against kin-slaying.

Lindow maintains this interpretation in spite of his own concession that, so far as the Eddic attestations of the Baldr narrative are concerned, "the textual tradition does not suggest it [i.e., kin-slaying] as inherently problematic; for example, Snorri calls Váli *happskeytr*, and kin-slaying is just the sort of thing that one would ordinarily regard as *óhapp*."[87] Many of Lindow's assumptions about the feud are drawn from anthropological studies such as Christopher Boehm's *Blood Revenge* (1987). While Boehm does indeed assert that kin-slaying was necessarily incompatible with the requirements of the bloodfeud since it diminished the fighting capacity of an individual household, he does refer to at least one episode in which the restraint on intra-group vengeance was overridden by the duties of hospitality. Boehm alludes to an anecdote from the Serbian author Marko Miljanov's memoirs about an Albanian "who killed his own brother because the latter had killed a houseguest."[88] According to Boehm, this tale "exemplifies a rule that also held strongly in Montenegro" and is probably characteristic of multiple feuding societies.

Any assertion that the pursuit of vengeance within the kin group was categorically prohibited in the world of *Beowulf*

---

[86] *Beowulf*, ll. 588-89. See John Lindow, *Murder and Vengeance among the Gods: Baldr in Scandinavian Mythology*, FF Communications 262 (Helsinki: Academia Scientiarum Fennica, 1997), p. 143.

[87] John Lindow, "Bloodfeud and Scandinavian Mythology," *alvíssmál* 4 (1994 [1995]), pp. 51-68 at p. 64 n. 16.

[88] Christopher Boehm, *Blood Revenge: The Enactment and Management of Conflict in Montenegro and Other Tribal Societies* (Philadelphia: University of Pennsylvania Press, 1984 repr. 1987), p. 119.

would have to be reconciled with episodes from Germanic literature indicating precisely the opposite situation. The most famous narrative of vengeance in Germanic literature—that of Saxo's Amleth—culminates in an act of kin-slaying about which Saxo clearly felt no misgivings. It is because Amleth stabbed his uncle to death that Saxo considers him "[f]ortem virum æternoque nomine dignum" ("a great man worthy of an eternal name").[89]

The words with which Saxo concludes the tale leave no doubt that vengeance within the kin was, at least in this case, wholly acceptable to the author: "Itaque et se sollerter tutatus et parentem strenue ultus, fortior an sapientior existimari debeat, incertum reliquit" ("Given the skill with which he kept himself safe and the energy with which he avenged his father, it remains uncertain what one should praise more, his strength or his wisdom"). According to J. M. Wallace-Hadrill's discussion of feuding within the Merovingian royal household, it was "propinquity of blood" and not the implicit norms of the bloodfeud that most often led warring parties toward settlement: certainly it was not of itself able to prevent intra-group feuds from occurring.[90] While there can be no doubt that families preferred not to fight among themselves, the abundance of contradictory evidence in England and on the Continent makes an abhorrence for vengeance within the kin difficult to establish as a Pan-Germanic custom.

Arguments by Bertha Phillpotts suggest that the bonds of kinship may themselves have been exaggerated in nineteenth and early twentieth-century studies of *Beowulf.* From *Beowulf,* Phill-

---

[89] *Saxonis Gesta Danorum,* eds. C. Knabe, P. Hermann, J. Olrik and H. Ræder, 2 vols. (Copenhagen: Levin & Munksgaard, 1931), I, 84 (3.6.25).

[90] J. M. Wallace-Hadrill, "The Bloodfeud of the Franks," *Bulletin of the John Rylands Library* 41 (1959); repr. in idem, *The Long-Haired Kings,* Medieval Academy Reprints for Teaching 11 (Toronto: Univ. of Toronto Press, 1982), pp. 121-147 at p. 131.

potts contends, "we glean nothing that can serve as evidence for kin-solidarity."[91] Phillpotts goes on:

> On the contrary, we find Hrôðgâr, a foreign king, paying com-
> pensation on behalf of Ecgþeow for his slaying of Heaðolâf,
> one of the Wylfing dynasty (l. 470 f.). And from the passage
> which describes Hrôðgâr indemnifying with rich gifts the com-
> panions of Aeschere, who had been slain by Grendel's mother
> (ll. 1053 ff.), we can only assume that it was the members of the
> comitatus rather than the kin, who received wergeld for a war-
> rior slain in his lord's employ.[92]

Phillpotts finds further evidence for the lack of kin-solidarity in the famous *Anglo-Saxon Chronicle* entry for the year 755
containing the Cynewulf and Cyneheard narrative. When Cyneheard points out to the followers of the slain king Cynewulf that
they will be fighting against their own kin should they pursue
vengeance on his behalf, Cynewulf's *comitatus* replies "þæt him
nænig mæg leofre nære þonne hiera hlaford" ("that to them no
kinsman was dearer than their lord").[93]

According to Charles Plummer, it is here that "the tie of the
comitatus supersedes that of the kin; the comitatus forms as it
were an artificial family with its leader as 'father and lord.'"[94]

---

[91] Bertha Phillpotts, *Kindred and Clan in the Middle Ages and After. A Study
in the Sociology of the Teutonic Races* (Cambridge: Cambridge Univ. Press,
1913), pp. 236-37.

[92] Phillpotts, *Kindred and Clan*, p. 237.

[93] Plummer and Earle, *Two of the Saxon Chronicles*, I, 48.

[94] Plummer and Earle, *Two of the Saxon Chronicles*, II, 46-47. Phillpotts additionally
notes "the violation of the old rule that there should be no wergeld within
the kindred" in Archbishop Theodore's mediation of a dispute in 679
between kings Egfrid and Ethelred over the death of Egfrid's brother Elfwin.
The deceased was a brother-in-law to Ethelred, who had married Elfwin's
sister Osthryd, yet Theodore arranged for a successful pecuniary settlement
in which Ethelred paid *wergeld* to Egfrid. The possibility of such a settlement

Brunner was probably right to suggest that vengeance might take place within the kin group, and that for this reason Hrethel might not have violated the protocols of his own culture in taking Hæthcyn's life, should Hæthcyn's offense have been viewed as tantamount to deliberate homicide. The inevitable question we are left with, as Seebohm's comments suggest, is why Hrethel abstains from any violent reprisals. This chapter establishes that the most convenient explanation for Hrethel's inaction inheres not in his status within the kin group but in the accidental nature of Hæthcyn's offense itself. No vengeance was pursued because, in cases of accident, no vengeance was called for. Accidental homicides could initiate further acts of vengeance only when their accidental status came into doubt. Beowulf's own comments, often construed as indicating his unrequited desire for vengeance, are perhaps best seen as lamenting the fact of unavenged death itself, undoubtedly a grievous event in a social environment where vengeance and settlement were the predominant modes of dispute resolution. Vengeance might remain a craving, as it certainly appears to have been for Beowulf, and perhaps was for his foster-father as well. It seems clear, nonetheless, that the implicit norms governing the behavior of disputants in the world of *Beowulf* would have forbidden any lethal reprisals, much as they appear to have done in most Germanic legislation.

offers reasons to doubt the standard claim that Herebeald's death was *feohleas* because there could be no payments of *wergeld* within the kin. *See* Phillpotts, *Kindred and Clan*, p. 238.

# Conclusions

## LAW AND THE ARCHAISM OF *Beowulf*

I WOULD LIKE TO CONCLUDE THIS STUDY with some remarks concerning the "archaism" of *Beowulf,* an issue that should be distinguished from the problem of the poem's date. I believe that it is in discussions of the degree to which *Beowulf* exemplifies "archaic" attitudes characteristic of early Germanic-speaking peoples that we encounter one of the most persistent legacies of nineteenth-century legal-historical scholarship—one whose relevance to the state of present-day scholarship on Old English is considerable.

It is useful to keep in mind that, due to the dominance of the *Liedertheorie* and allied theories of composite authorship throughout much of the nineteenth century, questions of dating had a kind of fluidity in the first several decades of *Beowulf*'s reception that one does not find in most scholarship of the twentieth century. Proposed dates of composition varied widely, and the question of dating itself involved situating all of the poem's components into an imagined chronology. Consequently, while contemporary arguments for an early date would place the poem somewhere during the eighth century, scholars of the early nineteenth century often held that many of the poem's components had circulated (perhaps independently) in the earliest phases of Germanic prehistory.[1]

This complicated picture—familiar to all students of *Beowulf*'s reception history—was made more complicated by a development discussed in chapter 1, Grimm's use of the poem to demonstrate the poetic origins of all Germanic legal observances. The ensuing arguments that *Beowulf* contained traces of early

---

[1] See Chase, "Opinions on the Date of Beowulf," pp. 3-4.

Germanic lawmaking in effect placed parts of the poem having to do with law beyond the scope of chronological analysis. The fundamental assumptions of Grimm and his followers about the institutional setting of *Beowulf* were passed on to twentieth-century scholars even as the theories of composite authorship that made these assumptions possible fell out of favor.

One of the legacies of Grimm's "discovery" that can thus be found in most editions of *Beowulf* and a fair amount of the scholarship as well is the tendency to resolve questions concerning the poem's legal setting not with sources that are chronologically closer to the poem (such as Bede's "Letter to Egbert") but with references to Tacitus's *Germania*. Discussions of law in our major editions frequently show little interest in the question of whether Germanic institutions display chronological change, since for most of the poem's major editors, Germanic law remained as it had been for Grimm and Brunner, "a system inherent in society's soul."[2] Law was implicitly held to be unchanging in its most essential aspects from the earliest to the latest surviving evidence. Legal matters in Klaeber's edition, for example, are more frequently explained with allusions to abstractions such as "Germanic custom" and the "heroic code" than to any record of Anglo-Saxon legislation or dispute settlement.

The dominance of Klaeber's edition ensured that later scholarship would adopt this approach in a nearly uncritical fashion when addressing legal-historical problems within the poem. Little interest was shown in relating the contents of *Beowulf* to the legislative records of the various Germanic-speaking peoples because, as I have argued in chapter 1, this legislative record was widely seen as already having been corrupted by the influence of Christianity and the remains of Roman law. *Beowulf* was supposed to bear less of this taint, and it was for this reason that scholars like Brunner made legislative evidence subordinate to that of literature in determining the legal status of accidental wrongs in Germanic society.

---

[2] Wormald, *Making of English Law*, p. 23.

The critical habits described above are similar to those identified by Allen Frantzen in his wide-ranging discussion of how
present-day medieval studies reproduce the ideology of nineteenth-century scholarship. Frantzen has observed that among
the most significant problems facing contemporary scholarship
on Old English are its habitual "[a]ppeals to consensus and authority," a tendency that has "badly . . . served the subject."[3] In
place of such appeals, Frantzen urges specialists in Old English "to examine the cultural and social constructions excluded
by narrow documentary analysis . . . to situate texts in a timely
rather than timeless sense."[4] Though Frantzen does not discuss
the legacies of early legal history specifically, it is clear that statements about the nature of early Germanic law that one often
finds in the major editions of *Beowulf*—e.g., "The ancient Germans held their lands in common," "Germanic peoples punished accidental and deliberate homicide with equal severity"—
are of the very type that Frantzen inveighs against throughout
his important study. They are peremptory statements of "objective" fact about materials that offer few grounds for real cer-
tainties, "agent[s] of closure, shutting off human investigation,
criticism, and effort."[5] The student of *Beowulf*, happening upon
such observations in the standard editions of the poem, is given
a series of static solutions to complex problems; solutions whose
form precludes what would seem to be obvious and necessary
questions regarding the authority of these claims.

The disembodied afterlife of the legal-historical doctrines
established by Grimm, Brunner and others in editions of *Beowulf*
they influenced allowed many of their observations on the poem
to avoid critical scrutiny while still furnishing the social background necessary to its critical exegesis throughout the twenti-

---

[3] Frantzen, *Desire for Origins*, p. 202.

[4] Frantzen, *Desire for Origins*, p. 201.

[5] Frantzen, *Desire for Origins*, p. 201. The passage itself is a quotation from
Edward Said, *The World, the Text, and the Critic* (Cambridge, MA: Harvard
Univ. Press, 1983), p. 290.

151

eth century. In the end, a number of these doctrines, many of which have long been the basis of the "appeals to consensus" deplored by Frantzen, might have been abandoned much sooner had philological scholarship on *Beowulf* not lost touch so completely with its roots in legal history. Such a conjecture seems especially plausible when one compares the relatively brief career of Kemble's hypothesis regarding the meaning of *folcland* with its inordinately long afterlife in *Beowulf* studies. Law appears to have been yet another area in which *Beowulf* scholarship was constrained to repeat the scholarly conventional wisdom without inquiring into its merits.

The present study hopefully will contribute to the efforts of present-day *Beowulf* scholarship to see some of its most basic assumptions in the "timely rather than timeless sense" advocated by Frantzen. It will also, I hope, provoke some consideration of the hazards entailed by our continued dependence on the theoretical models of Grimm and his descendants. Indeed, it could be argued that the very premises by which comparative philology first offered itself as a capable judge of legal-historical problems supply us with fairly simple criteria by which we can evaluate the soundness of its accomplishments. We know, for example, that the absorption of traditional legal history by comparative philology began with the powerful insight that law was as basic to human interaction as language. As such, it could be investigated, and its earlier manifestations reconstructed, using analogous methods of inquiry.[6]

How well, we might ask, did comparative philology keep its promise to bring to legal history the methodological discipline of comparative grammar? Naturally, if legal systems behave similarly to languages, it would seem to follow that they are subject to some of the most basic "laws" under which language can be demonstrated to operate. The sociolinguist Rosina Lippi Green has identified a number of rules that all linguists would agree govern the behavior of languages. Among these are the rules

[6] Wormald, *Making of English Law*, p. 11.

that "all spoken languages change over time," that "all spoken languages are equal in linguistic terms," and that "variation is intrinsic to all spoken language at every level."[7] These rules might also be applied to the study of customary law, which likewise can safely be assumed to change over time, to serve the purposes of those who employ it adequately in comparison with the customary observances of other groups, and to display a fair amount of variation among geographically disparate members of the same community. None of these statements appears to govern the discussions of legal matters in most scholarship on *Beowulf*. Over the last two centuries there has been little interest in observing variation among the legal customs of discrete Germanic-speaking communities. There has been tremendous interest in distinguishing the legal practices of early Germans from their Roman predecessors, a tradition that began in historiography as early as the sixteenth century, and which was ardently pursued by the first "scientific" students of language in England, Thorpe and Kemble, often as a means of demonstrating the inferiority of Roman and civil law.

The most characteristic and most damaging habit of Germanist legal history has been its abiding tendency to ignore the question of the chronological development of pre-conquest Anglo-Saxon law, juxtaposing instead its literate remains with those of Scandinavia in order to establish an abstract, timeless system of archaic Germanic law that dwelt in the national spirit of all Germanic-speaking peoples. While it is due in part to the bifurcation of legal and literary history, the 'static' character of legal-historical observations in Germanist scholarship (and hence in *Beowulf* scholarship) is also an unfortunate result of the polemical exchanges in which Grimm and his contemporaries were engaged concerning the equality of Roman and Germanic legal systems.[8] Above all, Grimm's argument for the poetic and

---

[7] Rosina Lippi-Green, *English with an Accent: Language, Ideology, and Discrimination in the United States* (London: Routledge, 1997), pp. 3-7.

[8] On the nature of the debate, see Wormald, *Making of English Law*, p. 11.

therefore "timeless" and archaic nature of Germanic law was an expedient; it was a means of artificially augmenting with examples from literature the otherwise sparse and disappointing scraps of legislative evidence available to scholars who aimed to establish the dignity and complexity of Germanic legal institutions alongside their Roman counterparts.

This study thus offers further grounds for agreement with Frantzen's contention throughout his *Desire for Origins* that much of the legacy of nineteenth-century scholarship is, in spite of its pretensions of scientific rigor and objectivity, ultimately derivative of nationalist and—in the case of some British scholarship—imperialist ideologies, and that for this reason the future relevance of Anglo-Saxon studies within the academy will depend upon its ability to exorcise these influences from its scholarly outlook. These are not trivial concerns, particularly given the bellicose nationalism and authoritarianism that have come to dominate the public sphere in the years since Frantzen's study was first published. In some ways, Frantzen's analyses of nineteenth-century British scholarship have acquired a new immediacy, as academic work once again must refuse at its own peril the imperative to reproduce the ideological conditions of empire.

In stating my agreement with the basic assumptions of Frantzen's study and many of those that have issued from it, I would, however, like to offer one caveat.[9] One of the hazards of the iconoclastic stance adopted by Frantzen is that it can turn, once having itself been adopted as an element of the scholarly consensus, into a reflexively dismissive attitude toward the work

---

[9] A convenient overview of the role of nineteenth-century and present-day nationalisms in shaping the critical reception of *Beowulf* can be found in Alfred David, "The Nationalities of *Beowulf*: Anglo-Saxon Attitudes," in *Beowulf in Our Time: Teaching Beowulf in Translation*, Old English Newsletter *Subsidia*, vol. 31, ed. Mary K. Ramsey (Kalamazoo, MI: The Medieval Institute, 2002), pp. 3-22. I am grateful to Professor David for supplying me with a copy of this essay.

of those who established Germanic philology as an independent discipline, leading some scholars to hold in suspicion even the methods and traditions of philology itself. Philology came in for a lot of abuse both before and since Frantzen's study, its diminished reputation due in no small part to the negative attention it received in Edward Said's *Orientalism*.[10] It is not my intention to contribute to the further marginalization of philology (implicitly defined throughout this study as the reconstructive and linguistically-oriented study of premodern literatures and cultures), which in the past two decades has often been either woefully misunderstood or employed as a metonym for all the retrograde tendencies of literary scholarship.

Nor has it been my purpose, even when taking issue with some of their claims, to malign scholars such as Grimm, Kemble and Brunner, or to trivialize the importance of their contributions to our knowledge of Germanic legal history, nor would I impute similar motives to other scholars who have addressed the role of nationalism in the formation of Old English studies. Work that has gone without any serious critical attention for over a century will inevitably reveal major weaknesses once it does receive such an examination. But it is humbling to remember that the conclusions of these scholars, however much they are conditioned by the fixations and ideological struggles of their own era, emerge from a period in which the province of philological study was much more expansive than it is today. In ascertaining the limits of their perspectives, it is worth keeping in mind that the field of vision of present-day English studies has itself become depressingly limited, both as a result of departmentalization and increased pressure toward the adoption of narrow specializations.

---

[10] Edward Said, *Orientalism* (New York: Random House, 1979 repr. 1994), pp. 120-148. Of course, the status of philology within English departments began its decline long before the appearance of Said's monumental work: see William Riley Parker, "Where Do English Departments Come From?", *College English* 28 (1966-67), pp. 339-51.

That so much of present-day Old English scholarship is devoted to reminding us of the descent of contemporary critical practices implies a widespread desire to ensure that future scholarship not persist in the blind adherence to outmoded interpretive models. Such a desire does indeed motivate many of the arguments advanced within this study. But I believe that the burgeoning interest in Anglo-Saxonism also reveals an awareness that the future importance of Old English scholarship depends upon our reacquainting ourselves, whatever the outcome, with those who constructed the edifice we now occupy. And many of these scholars—in particular, Grimm and Brunner—commanded such an astounding body of knowledge that some amount of idolatry was an understandable—if ultimately hazardous—outcome of their achievements. Thus I hope that, in the process of correcting what I believe are a number of outdated assumptions regarding the legal setting of *Beowulf,* I have also shed light on an unexplored and important aspect of its critical reception.

# Works Cited

Aarsleff, Hans. *The Study of Language in England, 1780-1860*. Princeton: Princeton Univ. Press, 1967.

Acton, Lord [John Emerich Edward Darlberg]. *A Lecture on the Study of History, Delivered at Cambridge June 11 1895*. London: Macmillan, 1895.

Adams, Henry. "The Anglo-Saxon Courts of Law." In *Essays in Anglo-Saxon Law*, eds. H. Adams *et al.*, 1-54. Boston: Little, Brown and Co, 1876; rpt. 1905.

Allen, John. *Inquiry into the Rise and Growth of the Royal Prerogative in England*. London: Richard and John Edward Taylor, 1830; rpt. 1849.

Antonsen, Elmer. "Linguistics and Politics in the 19th Century: The Case of the 15th Rune." *Michigan Germanic Studies* 6 (1980): 1-16.

————. ed. 1990. *The Grimm Brothers and the Germanic Past*. Studies in the History of the Language Sciences 54. Philadelphia: John Benjamins, 1990.

Ayres, Henry Morgan. "The Tragedy of Hengest in *Beowulf*." *JEGP* 16 (1917): 282–95.

Bartels, Arthur. *Rechtsaltertümer in der angelsächsischen Dichtung*. Kiel: Chr. Donath, 1913.

Bately, Janet, ed. *MS A, The Anglo-Saxon Chronicle: A Collaborative Edition 3*. Cambridge: D. S. Brewer, 1986.

Bédier, Joseph, ed. *La Chanson de Roland*. Paris: H. Piazza, 1924.

Berkhout, Carl T. and Milton McC. Gatch, eds. *Anglo-Saxon Scholarship: The First Three Centuries.* Boston, MA: G.K. Hall, 1982.

Bethurum, Dorothy. "Stylistic Features of the Old English Laws." *Modern Language Review* 27 (1932): 263–79.

Beyerle, Franz. *Das Entwicklungsproblem im Germanischen Rechtsgang.* Deutschrechtliche Beiträge, Forschungen und Quellen zur Geschichte des deutschen Rechts, 10.2. Heidelberg: Carl Winter, 1915.

————. and Rudolf Buchner, eds. *Lex Ribuaria.* MGH Leges Sectio I. Hanover: Hahnsche Buchhandlung, 1954.

Birrell, Jean. "Common Rights in the Medieval Forest." *Past and Present* 117 (1987): 22-49.

Birrell, T. A. "The Society of Antiquaries and the Taste for Old English 1705-1840." *Neophilologus* 50 (1966): 107–111.

Bjork, Robert. "Nineteenth-Century Scandinavia and the Birth of Anglo-Saxon Studies." In *Anglo-Saxonism and the Construction of Social Identity,* eds. Allen Frantzen and John D. Niles, 111-32. Gainesville: Univ. Press of Florida, 1997.

———— and John D. Niles, eds. *A Beowulf Handbook.* Lincoln, NE: Univ. of Nebraska Press, 1997.

Black-Michaud, Jacob. *Cohesive Force: Feud in the Mediterranean and the Middle East.* Oxford: Blackwell, rpt. 1975.

Blackstone, William. *Commentaries on the Laws of England.* 4 vols. Eds. Stanley Katz *et al.* Chicago: Univ. of Chicago Press, 1979.

Bloomfield, Josephine. "Benevolent Authoritarianism in Klaeber's *Beowulf:* An Editorial Translation of Kingship." *Modern Language Quarterly* 60 (1999): 129–59.

Boehm, Christopher. *Blood Revenge: The Enactment and Management of Conflict in Montenegro and Other Tribal Societies*. Philadelphia: University of Pennsylvania Press, 1984; rpt. 1987.

Bosworth, Joseph. *An Anglo-Saxon Dictionary.*, rev. ed. T. Northcote Toller. London: Oxford Univ. Press, 1898; rpt. 1964.

Böttcher, H. "Blutrache." In *Reallexikon der germanischen Altertumskunde*, vol. 3, ed. Johannes Hoops *et al*, 96-98. Berlin: De Gruyter, 1978.

Bouterwek, Karl W. "Zur Kritik des Beowulfliedes." *Zeitschrift für deutsches Altertum* 11 (1859): 59–113.

Brodeur, Arthur. "The Climax of the Finn Episode." *University of California Publications in English* 3 (1943): 312-30.

Brunner, Heinrich. *Deutsche Rechtsgeschichte*. 2 vols. 2nd ed. Berlin: Verlag von Duncker & Humblot, 1906; rpt. 1961.

―――. "Über absichtslose Missethat im altdeutschen Strafrechte." In *Forschungen zur Geschichte des deutschen und französischen Rechtes*, 487-523. Stuttgart: Verlag der J.G. Cotta'schen Buchhandlung, 1890; rpt. 1894.

Buckland, William Warwick. *A Text-Book of Roman Law from Augustus to Justinian*. Cambridge: Cambridge Univ. Press, 1921.

Bugge, Sophus, ed. *Sæmundar Edda hins fróþa*. Christiania: P.T. Mallings Forlagsboghandel, 1867.

Burrow, J. W. "'The Village Community' and the Uses of History in Late Nineteenth-Century England." In *Historical Perspectives: Studies in English Thought and Society in Honour of J. H. Plumb*, ed. Neil McKendrick, 255-84. London: Europa, 1974.

Camargo, Martin. "The Finn Episode and the Tragedy of Revenge in *Beowulf*." *Studies in Philology* 78 (1981): 120-134.

Cameron, Angus. 1981. "A Reconsideration of the Language of *Beowulf.*" *Toronto Old English Series 6.* In *The Dating of Beowulf,* ed. Colin Chase, 33–75. Toronto University Press, 1981.

Chambers, R. W. *Beowulf: An Introduction to the Study of the Poem with a Discussion of the Stories of Offa and Finn.* 3rd ed. Cambridge: Cambridge Univ. Press, 1959.

————. and A. J. Wyatt, eds. 1952. *Beowulf with the Finnsburg Fragment* Cambridge: Cambridge Univ. Press, 1952.

Charles-Edwards, Thomas. "The Penitential of Theodore and the *Iudicia Theodori.*" *Archbishop Theodore: Commemorative Studies on his Life and Influence,* Cambridge Studies in Anglo-Saxon England 11, ed. Michael Lapidge, 141–174. Cambridge: Cambridge U. Press, 1995.

Chase, Colin. "Opinions on the Date of Beowulf, 1815-1980." *The Dating of Beowulf.* Toronto Old English Series 6. Toronto: Univ. of Toronto Press, 1981.

Clanchy, M. T. "Remembering the Past and the Good Old Law." *History* 55 (1970): 165–76.

Cook, Albert. "The Province of English Philology." *PMLA* 115 (1897; rpt. 2000): 1742–43.

Cooper, David. *The Lesson of the Scaffold.* Athens, OH: Ohio University Press, 1974.

Cosijn, P.J. *Aanteekeningen op den Béowulf,* trans. as *Notes on Beowulf,* Leeds Texts and Monographs n.s. 12, eds. and trans. Rolf H. Bremmer Jr. *et al.* Leeds: University of Leeds, 1991.

Cubbin, G. P., ed. *MS D, The Anglo-Saxon Chronicle: A Collaborative Edition 6.* Cambridge: D. S. Brewer, 1996.

Darlington, R., ed. *The Vita Wulfstani of William of Malmesbury.* London: Royal Historical Society, 1928.

David, Alfred. "The Nationalities of *Beowulf:* Anglo-Saxon Attitudes." *Beowulf in Our Time: Teaching Beowulf in Translation,* Old English Newsletter *Subsidia* 31, ed. Mary K. Ramsey, 3-22. Kalamazoo, MI: The Medieval Institute, 2002.

Davies, Wendy and Paul Fouracre, eds. *The Settlement of Disputes in Early Medieval Europe.* Cambridge: Cambridge Univ. Press, 1986.

Davoud-Oghlou, Garabed Artin. *Histoire de la législation des anciens germains.* 2 vols. Berlin: G. Reimer, 1845.

Day, David. *"Hafa nu ond geheald husa selest":* Jurisdiction and Justice in *"Beowulf."* Ph.D. Dissertation, Rice Univ., 1992.

———. "Hands across the Hall: The Legalities of Beowulf's Fight with Grendel." *JEGP* 98 (1999): 313-24.

———. *"Hwanan Sio Fæhð Aras:* Defining the Feud in *Beowulf."* *PQ* 78 (1999): 77-95.

de Looze, Lawrence N. "Frame Narratives and Fictionalization: Beowulf as Narrator." *Texas Studies in Language and Literature* 26 (1984): 145-56.

de Salis, R., ed. *Leges Burgundionum.* MGH Leges Sectio I vol. II. Hanover: Hahnsche Buchhandlung, 1892.

Dickins, Bruce. "John Mitchell Kemble and Old English Scholarship." *Proceedings of the British Academy* 25 (1939): 51-89.

Dobbie, Elliott Van Kirk, ed. *Beowulf and Judith.* ASPR, IV. New York: Columbia Univ. Press, 1953; rpt. 1965.

Dobozy, Maria. "The Brothers Grimm: Jacob Ludwig Carl (1785-1863); Wilhlem Carl (1786-1859)." In *Medieval Scholarship: Biographical Studies on the Formation of a Discipline, vol. 2: Literature and Philology,* ed. Helen Damico, 93-108. New York: Garland, 1998.

Donoghue, Daniel, ed. *Beowulf: A Verse Translation.* Trans. Seamus Heaney. New York: Norton, 2002.

Downer, L. J., ed. *Leges Henrici Primi.* Oxford: Clarendon, 1972.

Drew, Katherine Fischer, trans. *The Burgundian Code.* Philadelphia: Univ. of Pennsylvania Press, 1976.

Einarsson, Stefán. "A Bibliography of the Works of Frederick Klaeber." In *Studies in English Philology: a Miscellany in Honor of Frederick Klaeber,* ed. Kemp Malone and Martin B. Ruud, 477-85. Minneapolis: Univ. of Minnesota Press, 1929.

Eliason, Norman. "*Beowulf* Notes." *Anglia* 71 (1965): 1-34.

———. "Beowulf, Wiglaf and the Wægmundings." *ASE* 7 (1978): 95-105.

Finsen, Vilhjálmur, ed. *Grágás: Islændernes Lovbog i Fristatens Tid.* Copenhagen: Berlings bogtrykkeri. 1852.

Fowler, Roger. "A Late Old English Handbook for the Use of a Confessor." *Anglia* 83 (1965): 1-34.

Frantzen, Allen. *The Literature of Penance in Anglo-Saxon England.* New Brunswick: Rutgers Univ. Press, 1983.

———. *Desire for Origins: New Language, Old English, and Teaching the Tradition.* New Brunswick: Rutgers Univ. Press, 1990.

Fry, Donald K. *Finnsburh: Fragment and Episode.* London: Methuen, 1974.

Fulk, R. D. "Review Article: Dating *Beowulf* to the Viking Age." *PQ* 61 (1982): 341-59.

———. "An Eddic Analogue to the Scyld Scefing Story." *RES* n.s. 40 (1989): 313-22.

———. "Textual Criticism." *A* Beowulf *Handbook,* eds. Robert E. Bjork and John D. Niles, 35-54. Lincoln: Univ. of Nebraska Press, 1997.

———. and John C. Pope, eds. *Eight Old English Poems.* 3rd ed. New York: Norton, 2001.

Gade, Kari Ellen. "Hanging in Northern Law and Literature." *Maal og minne* (1985): 159-83.

Gautier, Léon. "L'Idée Politique dans les Chansons de Geste." *Revue de questions historiques* 8 (1968): 79-114.

Gay, Peter. *The Cultivation of Hatred.* New York: Norton, 1993.

Georgianna, Linda. "King Hrethel's Sorrow and the Limits of Heroic Action in *Beowulf.*" *Speculum* 62 (1987): 829-50.

Goebel, Jr., Julius. *Felony and Misdemeanour.* New York: Commonwealth Fund, 1937.

Goldman, Laurence. "Accident and Absolute Liability in Anthro-pology." *Language and the Law,* ed. John Gibbons, 51-99. London: Longman, 1994.

Green, Alexander. "The Opening of the Episode of Finn in *Beowulf.*" *PMLA* 31 (1916): 759-97.

Green, D. H. *Language and History in the Early Germanic World.* Cambridge: Cambridge University Press, 1998.

Green, Richard Firth. "Medieval Literature and Law." In *The Cambridge History of Medieval Literature,* ed. David Wallace, 407-31. Cambridge: Cambridge Univ. Press, 1999.

Greenfield, Stanley and Daniel Calder. *A New Critical History of Old English Literature.* New York: New York Univ. Press, 1986.

Grimm, Jakob. "Von der Poesie im Recht." *Zeitschrift für geschichtliche Rechtswissenschaft* 2 (1816): 25-99.

———. *Deutsche Rechtsalterthümer.* Göttingen: Dieterichsche Buchhandlung, 1828.

Gummere, Francis B. *A Handbook of Poetics, for students of English Verse.* Boston, MA: Ginn & Co, 1895.

———. *Germanic Origins: A Study in Primitive Culture.* New York: Scribner's, 1892.

———. *The Oldest English Epic.* New York: MacMillan, 1909; rpt 1923.

Halldórsson, Ólafur, ed. *Jónsbók. Kong Magnus Hakonssons Lovbog for Island.* Odense: Odense Universitetsforlag, 1970.

Harrison, James A. "Old Teutonic Life in *Beowulf.*" *Overland Monthly* 4 (1884): 14-24, 152-61.

Heinzel, Richard. "Moritz Heyne's *Beowulf. Mit ausführlichem Glossar herausgegeben* (fünfte Auflage)." *Anzeiger für deutsches Altertum und deutsche Literatur* 15 (1889): 189.

Heusler, Andreas. *Das Strafrecht der Isländersagas.* Leipzig: Duncker & Humblot, 1911.

Higham, N. J. *An English Empire: Bede and the Early Anglo-Saxon Kings.* Manchester: Manchester University Press, 1997.

Hill, Christopher. "The Norman Yoke." *Puritanism and Revolution,* 50-122. London: Secker and Warburg, 1958.

Hill, John M. *The Cultural World in* Beowulf. Toronto: Univ. of Toronto Press, 1995.

————. "The Ethnopsychology of In-Law Feud and the Remaking of Group Identity in *Beowulf:* The Cases of Hengest and Ingeld." *PQ* 78 (1999): 97-123.

Hollander, Lee M. "Review of Vilhelm Grönbech, *Vor Folkeæt i Oldtiden: I. Lykkemand ok Niding." JEGP* 9 (1910): 269-78.

Holmes, Oliver Wendell. *The Common Law.* Cambridge, MA: Harvard Univ. Press, 1881; rpt. 1963.

Holsinger, Bruce. "Vernacular Legality: The English Jurisdictions of the Owl and the Nightingale." In *The Letter of the Law: Legal Practice and Literary Production in Medieval England,* eds. Emily Steiner and Candace Barrington, 154-84. Ithaca, NY: Cornell Univ. Press, 2002.

Hoops, Johannes. *Kommentar zum Beowulf.* Heidelberg: Carl Winters, 1932.

Hough, Carole. "The Early Kentish 'Divorce Laws': A Reconsideration of Aethelberht chs. 79 and 80." *ASE* 23 (1994): 1-6.

Huebner, Rudolf. *History of Germanic Private Law.* Continental Legal History 4. Trans. Francis S. Philbrick. Boston: Little, Brown & Co, 1918.

Hurston, Zora Neale. "How It Feels to be Colored Me." In *I Love Myself When I Am Laughing . . . : A Zora Neale Hurston Reader,* ed. Alice Walker, 152-55. Old Westbury, NY: Feminist Press, 1928; rpt. 1979.

Hyams, Paul. "Feud in Medieval England." *Haskins Society Journal* 3 (1991): 1-21.

Immelmann, Rudolf. "Beowulf 303ff. und 3074f." *Englische Studien* 67 (1933): 325-39.

―――."Beowulf 3074f.: Nachprüfung." *Englische Studien* 68 (1933): 1-5.

Insley, J. "Folkland (Meaning and Discussion)." *Reallexikon der Germanischen Altertumskunde*, vol. 9, ed. Johannes Hoops *et al.*, 311-13. Berlin: De Gruyter, 1995.

Irving, Jr., Edward B. *A Reading of Beowulf.* New Haven: Yale Univ. Press, 1968.

Jacobson, Stephen. "Law and Nationalism in Nineteenth-Century Europe: The Case of Catalonia in Comparative Perspective." *Law and History Review* 20 (2002): 307-47.

Jón Jóhanneson, ed. *Austfirðinga sögur.* Íslenzk fornrit 11. Reykjavík: Hið íslenzka fornritafélag, 1950.

John, Eric. *Land Tenure in Early England.* London: Leicester University Press, 1960.

―――. "Folkland Reconsidered." *Orbis Brittaniæ and other studies,* 64-127. London: Leicester Univ. Press, 1966.

―――. *Reassessing Anglo-Saxon England.* Manchester: Manchester University Press, 1996.

Jolowicz, H.F. *Historical Introduction to the Study of Roman Law.* Cambridge: Cambridge Univ. Press, 1965.

Jones, George Fenwick. "Was Germanic *Blutrache* a Sacred Duty?" *Studia Neophilologica* 32 (1960): 218-27.

Jurasinski, Stefan. "*Reddatur Parentibus:* The Vengeance of the Family in Cnut's Homicide Legislation." *Law and History Review* 20 (2002): 157-80.

————. "Andrew Horn, Alfredian Apocrypha, and the Anglo-Saxon Names of the *Mirror of Justices*." Forthcoming.

Kemble, J. M. *John Mitchell Kemble's Review of Jakob Grimm's Deutsche Grammatik.* Old English Newsletter *Subsidia* 6. Binghamton, NY: CEMERS, SUNY-Binghamton, 1833; rpt. 1981.

————. *The Saxons in England.* 2 vols. London: Taylor and Francis, 1849; rpt. 1876.

————. ed. *Codex Diplomaticus Ævi Saxonici.* 5 vols. London, Sumptibus Societatis (English Historical Society), 1839-40.

————. ed. and trans. *The Anglo-Saxon Poems of Beowulf, the Traveller's Song, and the Battle of Finnes-burh.* London: William Pickering, 1837.

Kennedy, Alan. "Feuds." In *The Blackwell Encyclopædia of Anglo-Saxon England,* ed. Michael Lapidge, *et al.,* 182-83. Malden, MA: Blackwell, 2001.

Keynes, Simon. "The Cult of King Alfred the Great." *ASE* 28 (1999): 225-356.

Kiernan, Kevin. "Grendel's Heroic Mother." *In Geardagum* 6 (1984): 13-33.

————. Beowulf *and the Beowulf Manuscript.* Rev. ed. Ann Arbor, MI: Univ. of Michigan Press, 1997.

Klaeber, Fr. "Studies in the Textual Interpretation of *Beowulf.*" *MP* 3 (1905): 45-465.

————. "Observations on the Finn Episode." *JEGP* 15 (1914): 544-49.

————. ed. *Beowulf and the Fight at Finnsburg.* 3rd ed. with 1st and 2nd supplements. Lexington, MA: Heath. 1950.

Kliger, Samuel. *The Goths in England: A Study in Seventeenth and Eighteenth Century Thought.* Cambridge: Harvard Univ. Press, 1952.

Knabe, C., Hermann, P., Olrik, J. and Ræder, H., eds. *Saxonis Gesta Danorum.* 2 vols. Copenhagen: Levin and Munksgaard, 1931.

Koebner, Richard. "The Settlement and Colonization of Europe." In *The Cambridge Economic History of Europe I: The Agrarian Life of the Middle Ages,* ed. M.M. Postan, 1-90. Cambridge: Cambridge Univ. Press, 1966.

Krapp, George Philip, ed. *The Vercelli Book.* ASPR II. New York: Columbia Univ. Press, 1932.

Krusch, Bruno, ed. *Gregorii Episcopi Turonensis Miracula et Opera Minora.* MGH Scriptores Rerum Merovingicarum I. Hanover: Hahnsche Buchhandlung, 1885.

————. *Gregorii Episcopi Turonensis Libri Historiarum.* MGH Scriptorum Rerum Merovingicarum I. Hanover: Hahnsche Buchhandlung, 1950.

Kuhn, Hans. "Kriegswesen und Seefahrt." *Germanische Altertumskunde.* ed. Hermann Schneider, 98-122. Munich: C.H. Beck'sche Verlagsbuchhandlung, 1938; rpt. 1951.

Lambarde, William. *Archaionomia.* London: Roger Daniel, 1568; rpt. 1644.

Lapidge, Michael. "The Archetype of *Beowulf.*" *ASE* 29 (2000): 5-11.

————. *et al.,* eds. *The Blackwell Encyclopædia of Anglo-Saxon England.* Malden, MA: Blackwell, 2001.

Lawrence, W. W. "Beowulf and the Tragedy of Finnsburg," *PMLA* 30 (1915): 372-431.

———. "The Dragon and His Lair in *Beowulf.*" *PMLA* n.s. 26 (1918): 547-83.

Levy, Ernst. *West Roman Vulgar Law. The Law of Property.* Memoirs of the American Philosophical Society 29. Philadelphia: American Philosophical Society, 1951.

Liebermann, Felix, ed. and trans. *Die Gesetze der Angelsachsen.* 3 vols. Halle: Max Niemeyer, 1903-16.

———. *The National Assembly in the Anglo-Saxon Period.* Halle: Max Niemeyer, 1913.

Lindow, John. "Bloodfeud in Scandinavian Mythology." *alvíssmál* 4 (1994): 51-68.

———. *Murder and Vengeance among the Gods: Baldr in Scandinavian Mythology.* FF Communications 262. Helsinki: Academia Scientiarum, 1997.

Lippi-Green, Rosina. *English with an Accent: Language, Ideology, and Discrimination in the United States.* London: Routledge, 1997.

Loyn, H. R. *Anglo-Saxon England and the Norman Conquest.* London: Longman, 1962.

———. "Folkland (History)." *Reallexikon der Germanischen Altertumskunde,* vol. 9, ed. Johannes Hoops *et al.,* 311-12. Berlin: De Gruyter, 1995.

Maitland, Frederic William and Pollock, Sir Frederick. *The History of English Law before the Time of Edward I.* Cambridge: Cambridge Univ. Press, 1898; rpt. 1968.

Malone, Kemp. "The Finn Episode in *Beowulf.*" *JEGP* 25 (1926): 157-72.

Mason, Emma. *St. Wulfstan of Worcester c. 1008-1095.* Oxford: Blackwell, 1990.

Matthews, David. *The Making of Middle English, 1765-1910.* Medieval Cultures 18. Minneapolis: Univ. of Minnesota Press, 1999.

Meritt, Herbert Dean, ed. *Old English Glosses.* Modern Language Association of America General Series XVI. New York: Modern Language Association, 1945.

Mickel, Emanuel. *Ganelon, Treason, and the "Chanson de Roland."* State College: Pennsylvania State Univ. Press, 1989.

Miller, Thomas, ed. *The Old English Version of Bede's Ecclesiastical History of the English People.* EETS o.s. nos. 95, 96, 110, 111. London: Oxford Univ. Press, 1890-98; rpt. 1959-63.

Miller, William Ian. "Choosing the Avenger: Some Aspects of the Bloodfeud in Medieval Iceland and England." *Law and History Review* 1 (1983): 159-204.

————. *Bloodtaking and Peacemaking: Feud, Law and Society in Saga Iceland.* Chicago: Univ. of Chicago Press, 1990.

Möller, Hermann. *Das altenglische Volksepos in der ursprünglichen strophischen Form.* Kiel: Lipsius und Tischer, 1883.

Moore, B. "The Relevance of the Finnsburh Episode." *JEGP* 75 (1976): 317-29.

Mora, María José. "The Invention of the Old English Elegy." *English Studies* 76 (1995): 129-39.

————. and María José Gómez Calderón. "The Study of Old English in America (1776-1850): National Uses of the Saxon Past." *JEGP* 97 (1998): 322-336.

Müllenhoff, Karl. "Die Innere Geschichte des Beowulfs." *Zeitschrift für deutsches Altertum und deutsche Literatur* 14 (1869): 193-244.

———. *Die Germania des Tacitus erläutert,* Deutsche Altertumskunde IV. Berlin: Wiedmannsche Buchhandlung, 1990.

Müller, Johannes. *Das Kulturbild des Beowulfepos.* Studien zur englischen Philologie LIII. Halle an der Saale: Max Niemeyer, 1914.

Munske, Horst Haider. *Der germanische Rechtswortschatz im Bereich der Missetaten,* vol. 1. Berlin: Walter de Gruyter, 1973.

Myerov, Jonathan. "Lines 3074-3075 in *Beowulf:* Movement into Knowing." *Anglia* 118 (2000): 531-55.

Neckel, Gustav, ed. *Edda: Die Lieder des Codex Regius nebst verwandten Denkmälern.* 5th ed., rev. Hans Kuhn. Heidelberg: C. Winter, 1983.

O'Brien, Bruce. *God's Peace and King's Peace: The Laws of Edward the Confessor.* Philadelphia: Univ. of Pennsylvania Press, 1999.

O'Brien O'Keefe, Katherine, ed. *MS C: The Anglo-Saxon Chronicle: A Collaborative Edition 5.* Cambridge: D. S. Brewer, 2000.

Oliver, Lisi. "*Cyninges Fedesl:* The Feeding of the King in Aethelberht ch. 12." *ASE* 27 (1998): 31-40.

Orchard, Andy. *A Critical Companion to* Beowulf. Cambridge: D.S. Brewer, 2003.

Palgrave, Sir Francis. *A History of the Anglo-Saxons.* London: William Tegg, 1869.

Paul, Hermann. *Deutsches Wörterbuch. Bedeutungsgeschichte und Aufbau unseres Wortschatzes.* 10th ed., rev. Helmut Henne *et al.* Tübingen: Max Niemeyer, 2002.

Parker, William Riley. "Where do English Departments Come From?" *College English* 28 (1966-67): 339-51.

Pelteret, David A. E. *Slavery in Early Mediaeval England*. Woodbridge: Boydell, 1995.

Peterson, Sir William, ed. and trans. *Tacitus: Dialogus, Agricola, Germania.* Loeb Classical Library 35. Cambridge, MA: Harvard Univ. Press, 1914; rpt. 1946.

Phillpotts, Dame Bertha. *Kindred and Clan.* Cambridge: Cambridge Univ. Press, 1913.

―――. "Wyrd and Providence in Anglo-Saxon Thought." *Essays and Studies* 13 (1928): 7-27.

Plucknett, T. F. T. "Revisions in Economic History: III. Bookland and Folkland," *Economic History Review* 6 (1935): 64-72.

Plummer, Charles and John Earle, eds. *Two of the Saxon Chronicles Parallel.* 2 vols. Oxford: Clarendon, 1899.

Pocock, J. G. A. *The Ancient Constitution and the Feudal Law.* Cambridge: Cambridge Univ. Press, 1957; rpt. with retrospect 1987.

Reynolds, S. "Bookland, Folkland and Fiefs." *Anglo-Norman Studies* 14 (1992): 211-27.

Richardson, H. G. and Sayles, G. O. *Law and Legislation from Æthelberht to Magna Carta.* Edinburgh: Edinburgh Univ. Press, 1966.

Rivers, Theodore John, ed and trans. *The Laws of the Salian and Ripuarian Franks.* New York: AMS Press, 1986.

Robertson, A.J., ed. and trans. *Anglo-Saxon Charters.* Cambridge: Cambridge Univ. Press, 1939.

Ruggieri, Ruggero. *Il processo di Gano nella Chanson de Roland.* Florence: Sansini, 1936.

Said, Edward. *Orientalism.* New York: Random House, 1979; rpt. 1994.

———. *The World, the Text, and the Critic.* Cambridge, MA: Harvard Univ. Press, 1983.

Sawyer, P. H. *Anglo-Saxon Charters: An Annotated List and Bibliography.* London: Royal Historical Society, 1968.

Schmidt-Wiegand, Ruth. "Das sinnliche Element des Rechts. Jakob Grimms Sammlung und Beschreibung deutscher Rechtsalthertümer." In *Kasseler Vorträge in Erinnerung an den 200. Geburtstag der brüder Jacob und Wilhelm Grimm,* Schriften der Brüder Grimm-Gesellschaft Kassel e.V. 19, ed. Ludwig Denecke, 1-24. Marburg: Elwert, 1988.

Scragg, D. G. and Carole Weinberg, eds. *Literary Appropriations of the Anglo-Saxons from the Thirteenth to the Twentieth Century.* Cambridge: Cambridge Univ. Press, 2000.

Sedgefield, W. J., ed. *Beowulf.* Publications of the University of Manchester – English Series 11. Manchester: Univ. of Manchester Press, 1910.
Seebohm, Frederic. *The English Village Community.* 4th ed. London: Longmans, 1915.
———. *Tribal Custom in Anglo-Saxon Law.* London: Longmans, 1911.

Shaw-Taylor, Leigh. "Labourers, Cows, Common Rights and Par-liamentary Enclosure: the Evidence of Contemporary Comment c. 1760-1810." *Past and Present* 171 (2001): 95-126.

Shippey, Thomas. "Structure and Unity." *A Beowulf Handbook,* ed. Robert Bjork and John D. Niles, 149-174. Lincoln NE: Univ. Nebraska Press, 1997.

———. and Andreas Haarder, eds. and trans. *Beowulf: The Critical Heritage.* London: Routledge, 1998.

Sievers, Eduard. "Beowulf 3066ff." *Beiträge zur Geschichte der deutschen Sprache und Literatur* 55 (1931): 376.

Simmons, Clare A. *Reversing the Conquest: History and Myth in Nineteenth-Century British Literature*. New Brunswick: Rutgers Univ. Press, 1990.

———. *Eyes Across the Channel: French Revolutions, Party History and British Writing, 1830-1882,* Interdisciplinary Nineteenth-Century Studies 1. Amsterdam: Harwood, 2000.

Sohm, Rudolf. *Die Fränkische Reichs und Gerichtsverfassung.* Weimar: H. Böhlau, 1871.

Somner, William. *Dictionarium Saxonico-Latino-Anglicum.* London: Daniel White, 1659.

Spelman, Sir Henry and Dugdale, William. *Glossarium Archaiologicum.* London: Alicia Warren, 1664.

Stanley, E. G. "Hæthenra Hyht in *Beowulf.*" In *Studies in Old English Literature in Honor of Arthur G. Brodeur.* ed. Stanley Greenfield, 136-51. Eugene, Oregon: Univ. of Oregon Press, 1963.

———. "Two Old English Poetic Phrases Insufficiently Understood for Literary Criticism: *þing gehegan* and *seonoþ gehegan.*" In *Old English Poetry: Essays on Style,* ed. Daniel Calder, 67-90. Berkeley: Univ. of California Press, 1979.

———. "The Scholarly Recovery of the Significance of Anglo-Saxon Records in Prose and Verse: a New Bibliography." *ASE* 9 (1981): 223-62.

———. "The Continental Contribution to the Study of Anglo-Saxon Writings Up To and Including That of the Grimms." In *Towards a History of English Studies in Europe: Proceedings of the Wildsteig-Symposium, April 30-May 3, 1982,* eds. Thomas Finkenstædt and Gertrud Scholtes, 9-39. Augsberg: Universität Augsberg, 1983.

———. *In the Foreground:* Beowulf. Woodbridge: D. S. Brewer, 1994.

———. "Courtliness and Courtesy in *Beowulf* and Elsewhere in English Medieval Literature." In *Words and Works: Studies in Medieval English Language and Literature in Honor of Fred C. Robinson,* eds. Peter S. Baker and Nicholas Howe, 67-103. Toronto: Univ. of Toronto Press, 1998.

———. *Die angelsächsische Rechtspflege und wie man sie später aufgefaßt hat.* Munich: Verlag der Bayerischen Akademie der Wissenschaften, 1999.

———. "Beowulf." In *The Beowulf Reader,* ed. Peter Baker, 3-34. New York: Garland, 2000.

———. *Imagining the Anglo-Saxon Past: The Search for Anglo-Saxon Paganism and the Anglo-Saxon Trial By Jury.* Woodbridge: D. S. Brewer, 2000.

Stenton, F. M. *The Latin Charters of the Anglo-Saxon Period.* Oxford: Clarendon, 1955.

———. *Anglo-Saxon England.* 3rd ed. Oxford: Oxford Univ. Press, 1971.

Stephen, Sir Leslie and Lee, Sir Sidney, eds. *Dictionary of National Biography.* 22 vols. London: Oxford Univ. Press, 1949-50.

Strohm, Paul. "Postmodernism and History." *Theory and the Premodern Text.* Medieval Cultures 26, 149-64. Minneapolis: Univ. of Minnesota Press, 2000.

Strong, Archibald. *A Short History of English Literature.* London: Oxford Univ. Press, 1921.

Swanton, M. J. *Crisis and Development in Germanic Society 700-800: Beowulf and the Burden of Kingship.* Göppinger Arbeiten zur Germanistik 333. Göppingen: Kümmerle Verlag, 1982.

Sweet, Henry and T.F. Hoad, eds. *A Second Anglo-Saxon Reader: Archaic and Dialectal.* Oxford: Clarendon, 1978; rpt. 1998.

Tate, W. E. *The Enclosure Movement.* New York: Walker and Co, 1967.

Terrill, Richard J. "William Lambarde: Elizabethan Humanist and Legal Historian." *Journal of Legal History* 6 (1985): 157-78.

Thompson, E. P. *Customs in Common: Studies in Traditional Popular Culture.* New York: The New Press, 1993.

Thorpe, Benjamin. *Ancient Laws and Institutes of England.* London: Eyre and Spottiswoode, 1840.

———, ed. 1855 repr. *The Anglo-Saxon Poems of Beowulf, the Scop or Gleeman's Tale, and the Fight at Finnesburg.* London: Clarendon, 1875.

Tolkien, J. R. R. "*Beowulf:* The Monsters and the Critics." *Proceedings of the British Academy* 22 (1936): 245-95.

Toswell, M. J. "Tacitus, Old English heroic poetry, and ethnographic preconceptions." In *'Doubt Wisely': Papers in Honour of E. G. Stanley,* eds. M. J. Toswell and E. M. Tyler, 493-507. London: Routledge, 1996.

Turley, Richard Marggraf. *The Politics of Language in Romantic Literature.* New York: Palgrave MacMillan, 2002.

Tuso, Joseph, ed. *Beowulf.* Trans. E. Talbot Donaldson. New York: Norton, 1975.

Tylor, Sir Edward Burnett. *Primitive Culture. Researches into the Development of Mythology, Philosophy, Religion, Language, Art and Custom.* 2 vols. Boston: Estes & Lauriat, 1874.

Vann, Richard T. "The Free Anglo-Saxons: A Historical Myth." *Journal of the History of Ideas* 19 (1958): 259-72.

Vinogradoff, P. "Folkland," *English Historical Review* 8 (1893): 1-17.

———. "Transfer of Land in Old English Law." *Harvard Law Review* 20 (1906-07): 532-48.

Vollrath-Reichelt, Hanna. *Königsgedanke und Königtum bei den Angelsachsen bis zur Mitte des 9. Jahrhunderts.* Kölner Historische Abhandlungen, 19. Cologne and Vienna: Böhlau Verlag, 1971.

von Amira, Karl. *Grundriss des germanischen Rechts.* Grundriss der germanischen Philologie, 5. Strassburg: Verlag von Karl J. Trübner, 1913.

von Savigny, Friedrich Carl. "Vom Beruf unserer Zeit für Gesetzgebung und Rechtswissenschaft." In *Thibaut und Savigny,* ed. H. Hattenhauer, 95-192. Munich: Vahlen, 1913.

von Schaubert, Else. *Heyne-Schücking's* Beowulf. 16th ed. Paderborn: Verlag Ferdinand Schöningh, 1946.

von Schwerin, C. F, ed. *Lex Saxonum.* MGH Leges 4. Hanover: Hahnsche Buchhandlung, 1918.

von Schwind, Ernst. *Lex Baiwariorum.* MGH Legum Sectio I. Hanover: Hahnsche Buchhandlung, 1926.
von See, Klaus. *Altnordische Rechtswörter.* Hermæa, 16. Tübingen: Max Niemeyer, 1964.

Wallace-Hadrill, J. M. "The Bloodfeud of the Franks." *The Long-Haired Kings.* Medieval Academy Reprints for Teaching 11, 121-147. Toronto: Univ. of Toronto Press, 1959; rpt. 1982.

Watson, Alan, *et al.,* eds. *The Digest of Justinian.* Philadelphia: Univ. of Pennsylvania Press, 1985.

White, Stephen D. "Maitland on Family and Kinship." *The History of English Law: Centenary Essays on Pollock and Maitland.* Proceedings of the British Academy 89, ed. John Hudson, 91-114. Oxford: Oxford Univ. Press, 1996.

Whitelock, Dorothy. *The Audience of Beowulf.* Oxford: Clarendon, 1951; rpt. 1958.

———. "Beowulf 2444-2471." *Medium Ævum* 8 (1939): 198-204.

———. "Anglo-Saxon Poetry and the Historian." *Transactions of the Royal Historical Society* 31 (1949): 75-94.

———, ed and trans. *English Historical Documents vol. 1, c. 550-1042*. 2nd Ed. London: Eyre and Spottiswoode, 1979.

Whitman, James Q. *The Legacy of Roman Law in the German Romantic Era*. Princeton: Princeton Univ. Press, 1990.

Wilda, Wilhelm Eduard. *Das Strafrecht der Germanen*. Halle: C.A. Schwetschke und Sohn, 1842; rpt. 1960.

Wiley, Raymond A., ed. *John Mitchell Kemble and Jacob Grimm, A Correspondence 1832-1852*. Leiden: E.J. Brill, 1971.

———. *Anglo-Saxon Kemble: The Life and Works of John Mitchell Kemble, 1807-1857: Philologist, Historian and Archaeologist. Anglo-Saxon Studies in Archaeology and History* 1. Oxford: B.A.R, 1979.

———. "Grimm's Grammar Gains Ground in England, 1832-52." *The Grimm Brothers and the Germanic Past*, ed. Elmer Antonsen, 33-42. Amsterdam: John Benjamins, 1990.

Williams, Ann. "Land Tenure." In *The Blackwell Encyclopædia of Anglo-Saxon England*, ed. Michael Lapidge *et al.*, 277-78, 2001.

Williams, Robert Allan. *The Finn Episode in* Beowulf: *An Essay in Interpretation*. Cambridge: Cambridge Univ. Press, 1924.

Winterbottom, M. and Ogilvie, R. M., eds. *Cornelii Taciti Opera Minora*. Oxford: Clarendon, 1975.

Wormald, Patrick. "Frederic William Maitland and the Earliest English Law." *Law and History Review* 16 (1998): 1-25.

———. *The Making of English Law: King Alfred to the Twelfth Century.* London: Blackwell, 1999.

Wrenn, C. L. and Bolton, W. F., eds. *Beowulf.* 5th ed. Exeter: Univ. of Exeter Press, 1996.

Zeumer, Karl, ed. *Lex Visigothorum.* MGH Leges Sectio I. Hanover: Hahnsche Buchhandlung, 1935.

# Index

Aarsleff, Hans, 1, 16-17
Acton, Lord [John Emerich Edward
Darlberg], 7
Adams, Henry, 7-8
Alfred of Wessex, 9
Allen, John, 20, 58, 60
Ayres, Henry Morgan, 79, 83, 103-104
Bartels, Arthur, 122-123
Bethurum, Dorothy, 16 n.37, 31
Beyerle, Franz, 67 n.49, 105
Black-Michaud, Jacob, 126, 131
Blackstone, William, 9-10, 57, 117, 137 n.71
Bloomfield, Josephine, 72
Boehm, Christopher, 145
Böttcher, H., 107
Bouterwek, Karl, 36, 38-39, 45
Brodeur, Arthur, 82, 102-103
Brunner, Heinrich, 20-21, 31 n.17, 33 n.21, 95, 107 n.88, 110, 115-123, 126-130, 132-36, 137 n.71, 140-143, 148, 150-151, 155
Burrow, J. W., 60 n.32, 129 n.52
Camargo, Martin, 79
Cameron, Angus, 86 n.28
Chambers, R. W., 37-38, 82-83, 88-89, 128
Chanson de Roland, 96-97

Charles-Edwards, Thomas, 142
Chase, Colin, 13 n.31, 96, 149 n.1
Clanchy, M. T., 21 n.46, 125
Cnut, 87 n.31, 115, 141-142
Comparative philology, 7, 10, 16, 26, 152-153
Cook, Albert, 15, 108 n.90
Cosijn, P.J., 50, 102
David, Alfred, 154 n.9
Davoud-Oghlou, Garabed Artin, 138
Day, David, 32, 84
de Looze, Lawrence N., 124-125, 144
Dickins, Bruce, 1 n.1
Drew, Katherine Fischer, 138
Eliason, Norman, 49-50, 74 n.65
Evolutionism, 4, 7-8, 77, 95, 129, 132, 135, 143
*folcscaru*, 20, 54-57, 61-64, 66-67, 71, 75-76
Frantzen, Allen, 2-3, 5, 142 n.81, 151-152, 154-155
Fry, Donald K., 79 n.1
Fulk, R. D., 13 n.31, 38, 144 n.84
Gade, Kari Ellen, 116 n.12
Gautier, Léon, 96
Georgianna, Linda, 125
Gesta Danorum, 34, 120, 146

Printed in the United States
48153LVS00007B/364-450